# THE GOSPEL IN BRIEF
## — Leo Tolstoy —

Translated by Isabel Hapgood

Edited and with a preface by F. A. Flowers III

University of Nebraska Press
Lincoln and London

# Dedicated To The Memory
## Of
# Ludwig Wittgenstein

Manufactured in the United States of America

♾ The paper in this book meets the minimum requirements of American National Standard for Information Sciences—Permanence of Paper for Printed Library Materials, ANSI Z39.48-1984

First Bison Books printing: 1997

Most recent printing indicated by the last digit below

10    9    8    7    6    5    4    3

Library of Congress Cataloging–in–Publication Data

Tolstoy, Leo, graf, 1828–1910.
[Soedinenie, perevod i issledovanie chetyrekh Evangelii. English. Selections]
The Gospel in brief / Leo Tolstoy; translated by Isabel Hapgood; edited and with a preface by F. A. Flowers III.
p. cm.
Includes bibliographical references.
ISBN 0-8032-9432-8 (pbk.: alk. paper)
1. Tolstoy, Leo, graf, 1828–1910—Religion. 2. Bible. N. T.
Gospels—Paraphrases, English. I. Hapgood, Isabel Florence,
1850–1928. II. Flowers, F. A., 1955–   . III. Title.
BS2555.T6452213   1997
226'.06—dc21
96-47159
CIP

# — Contents —

# — Editor's Preface —

## I.

Leo Tolstoy (1828–1910), one of the world's great novelists, finished writing *War and Peace* in 1869 and *Anna Karenina* in 1877. Despite his success, fame, and fortune, Tolstoy was on the verge of suicide by the end of 1879.[1] He had come to believe that his life was empty and had no meaning. This culminated in a spiritual crisis, which marked a dramatic turning point in both his personal and literary lives.[2] Tolstoy soon began a spiritual journey, a journey that would last until his death in 1910.

## II.

Leo Nikolaevich Tolstoy was born in 1828 on his family's estate, Yasnaya Polyana, located in the Russian province of Tula. Born to power and privilege, Tolstoy received his early education from tutors and was raised in the Orthodox Christian faith. The young aristocrat entered the University of Kazan in

1844, leaving in 1847 without receiving a degree. He left his Christian beliefs behind as well.[3]

Tolstoy joined the Russian army in 1852 and fought bravely in the Crimean War. He left the army at the end of the war in 1856 and made two separate trips to Western Europe between 1857 and 1861. He subsequently took up residence at Yasnaya Polyana, which had by then become his personal estate. Tolstoy married Sophie Andreyevna Behrs in 1862 and spent the next fifteen years managing his vast holdings, fathering thirteen children, and writing his great masterpieces, *War and Peace* and *Anna Karenina*. Tolstoy's diaries, however, reveal an unhappy marriage.[4]

By 1879, Tolstoy, at age fifty-one, was so depressed he would not go hunting because he feared he would turn his gun on himself.[5] Like many others of his time, he believed that more knowledge would inevitably lead to the answer to his suffering. Accordingly, Tolstoy began reading in earnest both scientific and philosophical works. He also corresponded with many illustrious men of his day. Neither science, philosophy, nor others, however, provided any answers.

Unable to find comfort in either knowledge or the examples of those wealthy men around him, Tolstoy undertook an in-depth study of Buddhism, Islam, and Christianity. He ultimately came to the conclusion that the solution to "the problem of life" could be found in the words and teachings of Jesus—but only if those words were stripped of the official Church's distortions and dogma.[6] Tolstoy's crisis and gradual renewal are described by William James in *The Varieties of Religious Experience*.

Tolstoy, now a Christian, felt extremely ill at ease with

the artificial and privileged life he had been leading. His desire for material things and his own personal ambition now caused him great moral distress. As a result, Tolstoy, in an effort to live life as revealed through the words of Jesus, condemned violence, gave up tobacco, alcohol, and other luxuries and tried to live a humble life. He dressed simply and worked long hours in the fields with the peasants. By 1890, Tolstoy, unwilling to own property any longer, divided his large estate into equal shares to be distributed to his wife and nine living children.

### III.

From 1879 until his death in 1910, Tolstoy devoted his prodigious literary talents primarily to the production of a large number of works on religious, moral, and social themes. They include *My Confession* (1879), *What I Believe* (1884), *My Religion* (1884), *The Kingdom Of God Is Within You* (1894), and *What Is Religion And Of What Does It Consist?* (1902). Tolstoy also wrote *The Gospel In Brief* during this time of spiritual journey. Tolstoy's religious works attracted many followers, as well as fierce opposition. Some of those most vigorously opposed included members of his own family.[7] The Russian Orthodox Church excommunicated Tolstoy in 1901 because of his challenge to both the Church and the State.

Tolstoy believed that the existence of God could neither be proved nor disproved and that the meaning of life lay beyond the limits of our minds.[8] Tolstoy also believed that Church officials and official Church doctrine interfered with one's ability to live a relatively peaceful life on a daily basis without significant pain and suffering.[9] According to Tolstoy, the official Church held itself out as an institution for making life better when, in truth, it was an institution allowing men to lead false lives.[10] The Christian Church of late-nineteenth-century Russia, Tolstoy maintained, represented the same darkness and evil against which Jesus had struggled.[11] The official Church allowed believers to rationalize virtually any kind of inhumane treatment and yet still be assured of some sort of afterlife. But Jesus, Tolstoy wrote, did not teach this.[12]

Tolstoy observed further that the fundamental tenets of the Church created a society in which one could not determine whether a person was attempting to lead a Christian life simply by examining his or her actions.[13] The Church elevated belief and faith to some other sphere, separate and independent from life itself.[14] The Church, Tolstoy wrote, either ignored Jesus's teachings altogether or distorted them on the few occasions it did choose to consider them. This ambiguous moral framework resulted from the Church's theological focus on questions such as Jesus's divinity and the holiness of the Bible. Tolstoy, on the other hand, believed that the words and teachings of Jesus, when stripped of the official Church's distortions, dogma, and ritual, would not cause privation and suffering, but, instead, would actually put an end to almost all of the suffering humankind experiences on a daily basis.[15]

Despite his strong beliefs and vigorous efforts, however, Tolstoy, at age eighty-two, was unhappy and felt that he had failed to live his life as a true Christian should. Leaving home secretly one night in 1910, Tolstoy mysteriously disappeared. He died a few days later of natural causes in a small railway station in Astapovo on November 22, 1910. Thousands of people throughout the world mourned his death. Denied a religious funeral by the Church, Tolstoy was laid to rest on his estate at Yasnaya Polyana.

## IV.

Tolstoy's *The Gospel In Brief* is a work that Tolstoy extracted from a larger work. Both were banned by the Russian authorities and neither was published in Russia during his lifetime. Tolstoy's *The Gospel In Brief* was first published in Switzerland. The translation reproduced in this edition is taken from a book entitled *My Confession, My Religion, The Gospel In Brief*, published by Charles Scribner's Sons in 1922.

In *The Gospel In Brief*, Tolstoy fuses "the four Gospels into one," seeking "a solution to the problem of life and not of a theological or historical question." That is why Tolstoy "was indifferent to know whether Jesus Christ is or is not God, and from whom proceeds the Holy Spirit." In *The Gospel In Brief*, Tolstoy sets aside the questions upon which the Church had for so long focused, such as those relating to Jesus's genealogy, the divinity of Christ, miracles attributed to him, and the sacredness of the Bible. Tolstoy does not broach these issues because they do not constitute a part of Jesus's teachings. By setting such matters aside, Tolstoy is able to focus exclusively on the teachings of Jesus. The words and teachings of Jesus contained in *The Gospel In Brief* are based on Tolstoy's concentrated study and interpretation of the original Greek versions of the four Gospels, as opposed to later translations. Tolstoy's fusing of "the four Gospels into one" constitutes an effort to help humankind determine how to live in a chaotic and indifferent world.

# The Gospel In Brief

V.

Tolstoy's *The Gospel In Brief* had a profound impact on many of its readers, including one particular renowned reader of Tolstoy, Ludwig Wittgenstein (1889–1951), one of the most influential and yet elusive personalities in the history of modern philosophy.[16] During the early months of World War I, Wittgenstein's regiment participated in the absurdly incompetent Galician campaign, in which there were more than 600,000 casualties. The great suffering Wittgenstein witnessed made him feel completely alone and abandoned. Soon after arriving in Galicia, he found himself in a small bookshop in Tarnow, which contained just one book: *Tolstoy on the Gospels*.[17] He bought *The Gospel In Brief*, merely because there was no other, and started reading it on September 1, 1914. Wittgenstein began receiving benefits from the book almost immediately. He "read and re-read it, and thenceforth had it always with him, under fire and at all times."[18]

Tolstoy's *The Gospel In Brief* did indeed captivate Wittgenstein. He wrote in his diary that "I say Tolstoy's words over and over again in my head," and he was able to recite whole passages by heart.[19] Wittgenstein also recommended Tolstoy's book to anyone in distress, explaining to one such friend in 1915 that "this book virtually kept me alive . . . you cannot imagine what an effect it can have upon a person."[20] Wittgenstein's comrades referred to him as "the man with the gospels."[21]

Tolstoy's teachings, as Wittgenstein quickly learned, required man to renounce the flesh and the gratification of his own desires and will. Man must also make himself independent of outward circumstances in order to serve the spirit, which is in all men and which makes all men sons of God.[22] Wittgenstein tried to live the Tolstoyan ideal of a simple life until his death in 1951. One of his first steps after returning from the war was to give away the immense fortune he inherited upon his father's death in 1913. Thereafter, a great simplicity, at times even an extreme frugality, became characteristic of Wittgenstein's life.[23]

Both Wittgenstein and Tolstoy understood that the question of the meaning of life was not an academic question and that words were inadequate to explain the meaning of life. Tolstoy also understood that the meaning or "sense" of life could not be found in any individual passage of the Gospels. But Tolstoy did believe that a sense of life becomes clear through an inner understanding derived from the simplicity, clarity, and harmony contained in Jesus' teachings as a whole. *The Gospel In Brief* contributes to this process of understanding by emphasizing that one's well-being may well depend upon not what has happened in the world around him, but, rather, upon one's spiritual condition. Or, as Jesus said, the Kingdom of God "has neither time nor place, because the Kingdom of God, the one which I preach, is within you."[24]

F. A. Flowers III

NOTES

1. Leo Tolstoy, *A Confession and Other Religious Writings* (London and New York: Penguin, 1987), pp. 13, 30–31, 34.
2. Ibid., pp. 1, 11–12.
3. Ibid., p. 19.
4. Ibid., p. 9.
5. Ibid., p. 30.

6. Ibid., pp. 14–15.

7. Ibid., pp. 1, 9.

8. Ibid., pp. 14, 50, 52, 63.

9. Ibid., p. 171.

10. Ibid., pp. 12, 15, 57, 76.

11. Leo Tolstoy, *The Kingdom of God is Within You* (1894; reprint, Lincoln: University of Nebraska Press, 1984), p. 34.

12. Ibid., pp. 34–35.

13. Tolstoy, *A Confession*, pp. 19–20.

14. Ibid.

15. Ibid., pp. 12–14; Leo Tolstoy, *My Confession, My Religion, The Gospel In Brief* (New York: Charles Scribner's Sons, 1922), pp. 121, 160, 217–18, 238.

16. Ray Monk, *Ludwig Wittgenstein: The Duty of Genius* (New York: Free Press, 1990).

17. Brian McGuinness, *Wittgenstein: A Life. Young Ludwig 1889–1921* (Berkeley: University of California Press, 1988), p. 220.

18. Ibid.

19. Quoted in McGuinness, p. 221.

20. Quoted in Monk, p. 132.

21. Quoted in Monk, p. 116.

22. McGuinness, pp. 220–21.

23. G. H. von Wright, "Biographical Sketch," in *Ludwig Wittgenstein: A Memoir*, by Norman Malcolm (Oxford: Oxford University Press, 2d rev. ed., 1984), p. 10.

24. See page 62.

# — Tolstoy's Introduction —

This present book is extracted from a larger work, which exists in manuscript, and cannot be published in Russia. That work consists of four parts, namely:—

1. An account of that course of my personal life, and of my thoughts, which led me to the conviction that in the Christian teaching lies the truth.

2. An investigation of the Christian teaching—first, according to the interpretation of the Greek Church solely; then, according to the interpretation of the Churches generally, and the interpretation of the apostles, councils, and so-called "Fathers." Also, an exposition of the falsity in these interpretations.

3. An investigation of the Christian teaching, based,

not upon the above interpretations, but solely upon the words and deeds ascribed to Christ by the four Gospels.

4. An exposition of the real meaning of the Christian teaching, of the motives for its perversions, and of the consequences to which it should lead.

From the third of these parts this present volume is condensed. I have there effected the fusion of the four Gospels into one, according to the real sense of the teaching. I had no need to digress from the order in which each Gospel is written, so that in my harmonisation the transpositions of verses, rather than being more, are less numerous than in the greater part of those known to me. In my treatment of the Gospel of John there is no transposition, but all stands in the same order as in the original.

My division of the Gospel into twelve chapters (or six, since each pair of the twelve may be taken as one) came about spontaneously from the nature of the teaching. The following is the purport of the chapters:—

1. Man is the son of the Infinite Source of Being; he is the son of this Father, not by the flesh but by the spirit.
2. And therefore, man must serve the Source of his being, in the spirit.
3. The life of all men has a divine Origin. This Origin only is sacred.
4. And therefore, man must serve this Source of all

human life. This is the will of the Father.

5. Service of the Will of the Father of Life is life-giving.

6. And therefore, it is not necessary to life that each man should satisfy his own will.

7. This present life in time is the food of the true life.

8. And therefore, the true life is outside time; it is in the present.

9. Time is an illusion of life; the life of the past and the future clouds men from the true life of the present.

10. And therefore, one must aim to destroy the deception arising from the past and future, the life in time.

11. The true life is that now present to us, common to all, and manifesting itself in love.

12. And therefore, he who lives by love now, in the present, becomes, through the common life of all men, at one with the Father, the source, the foundation of life.

So that the chapters, in pairs, are related as cause and effect.

Besides these twelve chapters, this exposition includes—(a) The introduction of the first chapter of the Gospel of John, where the writer of the Gospel speaks, in his own name, as to the purport of the whole teaching; and (b) a portion of the same writer's Epistle (written probably before the Gospel); this containing the general sense to be derived from the preceding exposition.

These two parts are not essential to the teaching.

Although the former, as well as the latter of them, might be omitted without loss (the more so as they come in the name of John, and not of Christ), I have, nevertheless, kept them, because, to a straightforward understanding of the whole teaching, these parts, confirming each other and the whole, as against the strange commentaries of the Churches, yield the plainest evidence of the meaning to be put upon the teaching.

At the beginning of each chapter, besides a brief indication of the subject, I had put words from the prayer taught by Jesus to His disciples, such as corresponded with the contents of the chapter.

At the conclusion of my work I found, to my astonishment and joy, that the Lord's Prayer is nothing less than Christ's whole teaching, stated in most concise form, and in that same order in which I had already arranged the chapters, each phrase of the prayer corresponding to the purport and sequence of the chapters, as follows:—

1. Our Father,  Man is the son of the Father.

2. Which art in Heaven,  God is the infinite spiritual source of life.

3. Hallowed be Thy name,  May the Source of Life be held holy.

4. Thy kingdom come,  May His power be established over all men.

5. Thy will be done, as in heaven,  May His will be fulfilled, as it is in Himself.

| | |
|---|---|
| 6. So also on earth. | So also in the bodily life. |
| 7. Give us our daily bread, | The temporal life is the food of the true life. |
| 8. This day. | The true life is in the present. |
| 9. And forgive us our debts as we forgive our debtors. | May the faults and errors of the past not hide this true life from us. |
| 10. And lead us not into temptation, | And may they not lead us into delusion. |
| 11. But deliver us from evil. | So that no evil may come to us. |
| 12. For Thine is the kingdom, the power and the glory. | And there shall be order, and strength, and reason. |

In that large third part from which this work is condensed, the Gospel according to the four Evangelists is presented in full. But in the rendering now given, all passages are omitted which treat of the following matters, namely,—John the Baptist's conception and birth, his imprisonment and death; Christ's birth, and his genealogy; his mother's flight with him into Egypt; his miracles at Cana and Capernaum; the casting out of devils; the walking on the sea; the cursing of the fig-tree; the healing of sick, and the raising of dead people; the resurrection of Christ Himself; and, finally, the reference to prophecies fulfilled in His life.

These passages are omitted in this abridgment, because, containing nothing of the teaching, and describing only events which passed before, during, or after the period in which Jesus taught, they complicate the exposition. However one takes them, under any circumstance, they bring to the teaching of Jesus neither contradiction nor confirmation of its truth. Their sole significance for Christianity was that they proved the divinity of Jesus Christ for him who was not persuaded of this divinity beforehand. But they are useless to one whom stories of miracles are powerless to convince, and who, besides, doubts the divinity of Jesus as evidenced in His teaching.

In the large work, every departure from the ordinary version, as well as every comment added to the text, and every omission, is made clear, and proved by the comparison of the various versions of the Gospels, from the examination of contexts, and finally, by considerations, philological and other. But in the present abridged rendering, all these arguments and refutations of the false understanding of the Churches, as well as the minute notes and quotations, are omitted; because, however true and exact they may be in their places, they cannot carry conviction as to the true understanding of the teaching. The justness of a conception of this kind is better proved, not by arguing particular points, but by its own unity, clearness, simplicity, fullness, as well as by its harmony with the inner feelings of all who seek truth. Speaking generally, in regard to what divergence there is between my rendering and the Church's authorized text, the reader must not forget that it is a gross error to represent the four Gospels, as is often done, to be books sacred in every verse and in every syllable. The reader must not forget that Jesus never Himself wrote a book, as did, for instance, Plato, Philo, or Marcus Aurelius; that He, moreover, did not, as

# Tolstoy's Introduction

Socrates did, transmit His teaching to informed and literate men, but spoke to a crowd of illiterate men; and that only a long time after His death men began to write down what they had heard from Him.

The reader must not forget that a great number of such accounts have been written, from which, at first, the Churches selected three, and then another. Moreover, in selecting those which seemed to them the best according to the proverb, "No stick without knots," the Churches, out of the enormous heap of the Christian literature, have been forced to take in with their bargain a great many knots; so that the canonical Gospels contain nearly as many faulty passages as those Gospels rejected as apocryphal.

The reader must not forget that it is the teaching of Christ which may be sacred, but in no way can a certain measure of verses and syllables be so; and that certain verses, from here to here, say, cannot be sacred merely because men say they are so.

Moreover, the reader must not forget that these selected Gospels are, at any rate, the work of thousands of various brains and hands of men; that during centuries the Gospels have been selected, enlarged, and commented upon; that the most ancient copies which have come down to us, from the fourth century, are written straight on without punctuation, so that, even after the fourth and fifth centuries, they have been the subject of the most diverse readings; and that such variations in the Gospels may be counted up to fifty thousand. The reader must have all this present in mind in order to disengage himself from the opinion, so common among us, that the Gospels, in their present

---

shape, have come to us directly from the Holy Spirit. The reader must not forget that, far from it being blamable to disencumber the Gospels of useless passages, and to illuminate passages the one by the other, it is on the contrary, unreasonable not to do this, and to hold a certain number of verses and syllables as sacred.

On the other hand, I pray my readers to remember that, if I do not hold the Gospels to be sacred books emanating from the Holy Spirit, I yet less regard the Gospels as mere historical monuments of religious literature. I understand the theological as well as the historical standpoint on the Gospels, but regard the books myself from quite another. I pray the readers of my rendering not to be misled, either by the theological view, or by that other, so usual in our day among educated men, the historical view, neither of which I hold with. I consider Christianity to be neither a pure revelation nor a phase of history, but I consider it as the only doctrine which gives a meaning to life.

And it is neither theology nor history which has won me to Christianity; but just this, that, when fifty years old, having questioned myself, and having questioned the reputed philosophers whom I knew, as to what I am, and as to the purport of my life, and after getting the reply that I was a fortuitous concatenation of atoms, and that my life was void of purport, and that life itself is evil, I became desperate, and wished to put an end to my life. But after recalling to myself how formerly, in childhood, while I still had religious faith, life possessed meaning for me; and that the great mass of men about me, who hold to faith and are uncorrupted by wealth, possess the meaning of life: after all this, I was brought into doubt as to the justness of the reply given to me by the wisdom of men of my own station, and I tried once more to understand what answer it is that Christianity gives to those men who live a life with meaning. And I embarked upon the study of Christianity, as to what in this teaching guides the lives of men. I began to study that Christianity which I saw applied in life, and to make the comparison of this applied Christianity with the sources whence it percolates. The source of the Christian teaching is the Gospels, and there I found the explanation of the spirit which animates the life of all who really live. But along with the flow of that pure, life-giving water I perceived much mire and slime unrightfully mingled therewith; and this had prevented me, so far, from seeing the real, pure water. I found that, along with the lofty Christian teaching, are bound up the teachings of Hebraism and the Church, both of which are repugnant and foreign to the former. I thus felt myself in the position of a man to whom is given a sack of refuse, who, after long struggle and wearisome labor, discovers among the refuse a number of infinitely precious pearls. This man then knows that he is not blameworthy in his distaste for the dirt, and also that those who have gathered these pearls at the same time with the rest of the sackful, and who have preserved them, are no more to blame than himself, but, on the contrary, deserve love and respect.

I knew not the light, and I thought there was no sure truth in life; but when I perceived that only light enables men to live, I sought to find the sources of the light. And I found them in the Gospels, despite the false commentaries of the Churches. And when I reached this source of light I was dazzled with its splendor, and I found there full answers to my questions as to the purport of the lives of myself and others,—answers which I recognized as wholly harmonious with all the known answers gained among other nations, and to my mind, surpassing all other answers.

I sought a solution of the problem of life, and not of a theological or historical question; and that is why I was indifferent to know whether Jesus Christ is or is not God, and from whom proceeds the Holy Spirit. And it is just as unimportant and unnecessary to know when and by whom such and such a Gospel was written, and whether such and such a parable came from Jesus Himself or not. For me, the only important concern was this light, which, for eighteen hundred years, has shone upon mankind; which has shone upon me likewise, and which shines upon me still. But to know, more then this, how I ought to name the source of this light, what elements compose it, and what kindled it, I in no way concerned myself.

I might end this preface here if the Gospels were newly discovered books, and if the teaching of Jesus had not been, these eighteen hundred years, the subject of a continuous series of false interpretations. But today, to rightly understand the teaching of Jesus as He must have understood it Himself, it is indispensable to know the chief causes of these false interpretations. The prime cause of such false interpretations, which make it now so difficult for us to recover the true teaching of Jesus, is the fact that, under the cover of the Christian teaching, have been preached the teachings of the Church, which are made up from explanations of most contradictory writings, in which only a small part of the true teaching enters; even that being distorted, and adapted to the commentaries. The teaching of

Christ, according to this misinterpretation, is simply one link in the great chain of revelation which began with the world's beginning, and stretches into the Church of our own time.

These misinterpreters call Jesus God; but the recognition of His divinity does not make them recognize a greater importance in His words and teaching than in the words of the Pentateuch, the Psalms, the Acts, the Epistles, the Apocalypse, or even the decisions of the Councils and the writings of the Fathers.

And this false understanding allows no presentment of the teaching of Jesus which does not accord with the revelations which have preceded and followed Him; doing this with the purpose, not to make clear the meaning of the teaching of Jesus, but to harmonize, as far as possible, various writings which contradict each other; such as the Pentateuch, the Psalms, the Gospels, Epistles, Acts and, generally, all those which pass for sacred.

It is possible, indeed, to make a limitless number of such interpretations, having for object, not truth, but the reconcilement of those two irreconcilables, the Old and the New Testaments. And, in fact, the number of these is unlimited. This is the case with the Epistles of Paul, and with the decisions of the Councils (which last begin with the formula: "It is the will of us and the Holy Spirit"); and such, also, is the case with the decrees of popes and synods, and with all false interpreters of the thought of Jesus. All recur to the same gross sanctions of the truth of their reconcilements, affirming that these reconcilements are not the result of their personal thought, but a direct witness from the Holy Spirit.

Without entering upon an analysis of these different dogmatic systems, each of which pretends to be the only true one, we may, nevertheless, well see that all of them, beginning by holding sacred the multitude of writings which make up the Old and New Testaments, thereby impose upon themselves an insurmountable barrier to the understanding of the real teaching of Jesus; and out of this confusion necessarily results the possibility, and even the necessity, of an infinite variety of opposed sects.

The reconcilement of all the revelations can be infinitely varied, but the explanation of the teaching of one person, and one looked upon as a God, should, on the contrary, not give rise to any difference of sect. It is impossible there should be conflicting ways of interpreting the teaching of a God come down to earth. If God had so come down to reveal unfailing truth to men, at least He would have revealed it in such a way that all might understand; if, then, this has not been done, that is because it was not God who came; or if, indeed, the truths of God are such that God Himself cannot make them plain to mankind, how can men do so?

If, on the other hand, Jesus was not God, but only a great man, His teaching can still less engender sects. For the teaching of a great man is only great because it explains in a clear, understandable way that which others have set out obscurely, incomprehensibly. That which is incomprehensible in the teaching of a great man is not great. The teaching of a great man can, therefore, engender no sects. Only, then, this interpretation, which pretends to be a revelation from the Holy Spirit, and to contain the sole truth, raises up antagonisms and gives birth to sects. However much the sects of various religions may assure us that they do not condemn those of other sects, that they pray for union with them, and have no hate to them, it is not true. Never, since the time of Arius, has a single dogma arisen from other cause than the desire to contradict an opposing dogma.

To maintain that a particular dogma is a divine revelation, inspired by the Holy Spirit, is in the highest degree presumption and folly. The highest presumption, because there is nothing more arrogant than for a man to say, "What I tell you, God Himself says through my mouth." And the highest folly, because there is nothing more stupid than to reply to one who says that God speaks by his mouth, "God says quite the opposite, and by mine own mouth." But in this way reason all the Churches; and hence have been born, and are now being born, all the sects and all the evil brought, and being brought, into the world in the name of religion.

And yet deeper than this surface evil, all the sects cherish a second internal vice, which destroys in them any character of clearness, certainty, and honesty. It is this. While these sects present us with their false interpretations, as the last revelation from the Holy Spirit, they are careful never to precisely and decisively determine what is the very essence and purport of this revelation, which they profess is continued through them, and which they call "the Christian teaching."

All the sectarians who accept the revelation from the Holy Spirit, along with the Mohammedans, recognize Moses, Jesus, and Mohammed. The Churchmen accept Moses, Jesus, and the Holy Spirit. But to Mohammedanism, Mohammed is the last prophet, who alone has given the definite explanation of the two preceding revelations,—this is the last revelation, which explains all the preceding; and this one every true believer has before him. With the religion of the Churches it is quite otherwise. That also, like the Mohammedan, accepts three revelations, but in place of calling their religion by the name of their last revealer, that is, the "religion of the Holy Spirit," they maintain their religion to be that of Jesus, and refer themselves to His teaching. So that, in giving to us what are really their own doctrines, they pretend to rest them upon the authority of Jesus.

Those religions of the Holy Spirit which offer to us the last and most decisive of revelations, whether it be in the writings of the Apostle Paul or the decisions of such and such Councils, or the decrees of popes or patriarchs, ought to say so, and call their faith by the name of him who had the last revelation. And if the last revelation is by the Fathers of the Church, or a decree of the Patriarch of the East, or a papal encyclical, or the syllabus or the catechism of Luther or Philaretus, people should say so, and call their faith by this name; because the last revelation, which explains all the preceding, is always the most important one. But they decline to adorn their dogmatic systems with the names of these authorities, and, continuing to preach quite against Christ's own teaching, they persist in maintaining that Jesus has revealed their doctrine to them. So that, according to their teaching, Jesus declared that He, by His blood, redeemed our humanity, ruined through Adam's sin; that there are three Persons in God; that the Holy Spirit came down upon the apostles, and was transmitted to the priesthood by the laying on of hands; that seven sacraments are necessary to salvation; that communion must be in two kinds; and so on. They would have us believe that all this is part of the teaching of Jesus; whereas we shall there seek in vain even the least allusion to any such matters. The Churches which so pretend would do well in concluding to give all this to us at once as the doctrine of the Holy Spirit, not of Jesus; for, in short, only those are Christians who hold the revelation of Jesus Himself as the decisive one, in virtue of His own saying, that His followers must own no other master than Himself.

It would seem that the matter is so plain that it is not worth thinking about; but however strange it seems to say so, it is none the less true that up till now the teaching of Jesus is not separated, on the one hand, from artificial and unwarrantable connection with the Old Testament, and, on the other hand , from the superadded fantastic notions which have been imposed upon it under cover of the name of the Holy Spirit. Up to now, there are some who, in calling Jesus the second Person of the Trinity, will not conceive of His teaching otherwise than as in accordance with the so-called revelations of the third Person, as these are found in the Old Testament, the decrees of Councils, and the conclusions of the Fathers of the Church; and in preaching the most extravagant things, they affirm these extravagances to be the religion of Christ. Others there are who, in refusing to regard Jesus as a God, similarly conceive of His teaching, not at all as He Himself declared it, but as what Paul and the other interpreters have made of it. Whilst considering Jesus as a man, and not as a God, these learned men deprive Him of a common natural right: the right of being held responsible for His own words only, and not for the words of His misinterpreters. In their endeavors to elucidate the teaching of Jesus, they attribute to Him ideas which He never thought of uttering. The representatives of this school, the most popular of them, do not see it their duty to take the trouble of distinguishing between that which bears the stamp of Jesus Himself and that which His interpreters have wrongly ascribed to Him. And, instead of thus troubling to search out the teaching of Jesus Himself a little more deeply than the Churches have done, they have been led to seek in the events of His life, and in the facts of history contemporary with Him, the explanation of His influence and of the diffusion of His ideas.

The problem they are called upon to solve is, in effect, this—

Eighteen hundred years ago a poor wanderer appeared on earth who taught certain things. He was flogged and executed. And since then, although many and many just men have suffered for the belief, millions of people, wise and foolish, learned and ignorant, cannot shake off the conviction that this man, alone among men, was God. Here is a strange phenomenon; how is it to be explained? The Churches explain it by saying that this man, Jesus, was really God, by which everything is explained. But if this man was not God, how are we to explain why this mere man, in particular, has been acknowledged as God?

On this point the learned people of our schools of history gather with extreme care every detail of the life of this man, without noticing that, even though they should succeed in gathering a great number of these details (in truth, they have gathered none); and even though they should succeed in entirely reconstructing the life of Jesus in the smallest details, the supreme question remains unanswered,—the question as to why Jesus, and no one else, exercised such an influence over men. The answer to this is not found in knowledge of the society in which Jesus was born, brought up, and so on; still less is it found in knowledge of the happenings in the Roman world at about this time, or in the fact that the people were inclined to superstitious beliefs. To gain this answer, it is only needful to find what precisely was the especial mark of Jesus which has led so many people to raise Him above the rest of men, and, for eighteen hundred years, to hold Him as a God.

He who would solve this problem, it would seem, must, before all, bring himself to understand the teaching of Jesus: His true teaching, clearly seen, and not the crude interpretations which have been put upon it. But this is just what is neglected. The learned historians of Christianity are so satisfied to think that Jesus was no God, they are so keen to prove that His teaching holds nothing divine, and is, therefore, not binding, that they are not alive to a very plain fact: they do not see that, the more they prove Jesus to have been simply a man, and in nothing divine, the darker and more insoluble they make the problem they have in hand. They are making their full efforts to prove that He was simply a man, that, therefore, His teaching is not obligatory.

The essential thing is: not to prove that Jesus was no God, and His doctrine not divine, any more than to prove He was not a Catholic: but to know what His teaching essentially is; that teaching which has seemed to men so lofty and so precious, that they have again and again owned Him for God who gave it to them.

If the reader belongs to that vast body of educated men who have been brought up in the beliefs of a Church, and who have not renounced its absurdities; if he be a man of reason and conscience (whether retaining love and respect for the Christian teaching, or whether, following the proverb, "Burn the coat now the vermin have got in," he thinks the whole of Christianity a pernicious superstition), I pray him to reflect that that which shocks him, and seems to him a superstition, is not the real teaching of Jesus; and that it were unjust to make Jesus responsible for the follies which have, since His time, incrusted His teaching. It is only necessary to study the teaching of Jesus in its proper form, as it has come down to us in the words and deeds which are recorded as His own. With readers of the kind I have addressed, my book will go to show that Christianity is not only a mixture of things sublime and things base; that it is not only not a superstition, but that, on the contrary, it is the most convincing presentment of metaphysics and morals, the purest and most complete doctrine of life, and the highest light which the human mind has ever reached; a doctrine from which all the noblest activities of humanity in politics, science, poetry, and philosophy instinctively derive themselves.

If, on the other hand, my reader belongs to that small minority of educated men who remain attached to Church doctrines, and who accept religion, not for an outward end, but to gain inward quietude, then I ask such a reader to remember that the teaching of Christ, as set forth herein, is quite other than that teaching as he has been given to understand it; and that, therefore, the question for him is, not as to whether the doctrine here put before him agrees with his beliefs, but as to which is more in harmony with his reason and his heart—the teaching of his Church composed of reconcilements of many scriptures, or the pure teaching of Jesus. It concerns him only to decide whether he will accept the new teaching or whether he prefers to retain the teaching of his Church.

If, finally, my reader belongs to the category of men who value and accept outwardly the belief of some Church, not at all for truth's sake, but for the outward consideration of gains that come therefrom, such a one should inform himself that, whatever be the number of his coreligionists, whatever their power, whatever their station, even though monarchs, and whatever lofty personages they can reckon among them, he himself forms one of a party, not of the accusers, but of the accused. Such readers should inform themselves that they are not asked to furnish arguments for their case, because, this long while, all such arguments have been given which can be given; and even should they cite their proofs, they would only prove that which every one of the hundreds of opposing sects proves in its own case.

And, in truth, such people need not to prove anything, but to clear themselves, first, of the sacrilege they commit in putting the teaching of Jesus, whom they hold to be God, upon the same footing as the teachings of Ezra, of the Councils, of Theophylact; and in allowing themselves to distort the sayings of God into agreement with the sayings of men. Again, they must clear themselves of blasphemy in ascribing to God-Jesus all the zealotry which abides in their own hearts, and declaring it to be teaching of Christ. And finally, they must clear themselves of the treason they commit in hiding from men the teaching of God, who has come down to earth to bring us salvation; and by sliding in, to displace this teaching, the tradition of the Holy Spirit, thus depriving thousands of millions of that salvation which Jesus brought for men; and thus, instead of peace and love, bringing in all the diversity of sects, and all the recriminations, murders, and all sorts of misdeeds which follow.

For these readers there are only two issues: either to make humble submission, and renounce their deceits; or, to persecute those who arise to accuse them of the evil they have done and are doing.

If they will not renounce their deceits, it remains for them to take the only other part, that is, to persecute me. For which, in now completing my writing, I am prepared, with joy, and with fear for my own human weakness.

# — The Gospel In Brief —

# 1

## Our Father
### The Son Of God The Spirit

*Man, the son of God, is powerless in the flesh,
and free in the spirit.*

THE BIRTH OF JESUS CHRIST was thus:— <sub></sub> Mt. I. 18
His mother Mary was betrothed to Joseph. But,
before they began to live as man and wife, Mary 19
proved with child. But Joseph was a good man,
and did not wish to disgrace her; he took her as 24
his wife, and had nothing to do with her until she 25
had borne her first son, and called him Jesus.

And the boy grew and matured, and was Lk. II. 40
intelligent beyond his years.

Jesus was twelve years old; and it hap- 41
pened that Mary and Joseph went to the feast at 42
Jerusalem, and took the boy with them. The 43
feast was over, and they went homeward, and 44

forgot about the boy. Afterward they recollected, and thought that he had gone off with the children, and they inquired about him along the road. He was nowhere to be found, and they went back to Jerusalem after him. And it was the third day before they found the boy in the temple, sitting with the teachers, questioning them, and listening. And every one wondered at his intelligence. His mother caught sight of him, and said: "Why have you done this way with us? Your father and I have been grieving, and looking for you." And he said to them: "But where did you look for me? Surely you ought to know that the son must be looked for in his Father's house?" And they did not understand his words; they did not understand whom it was he called his Father.

And after this, Jesus lived at his mother's and obeyed her in everything. And he advanced in age and intelligence. And everyone thought that Jesus was the son of Joseph; and so he lived to the age of thirty.

At that time the prophet John appeared in Judea. He lived in the desert of Judea, on the Jordan. John's clothes were of camel's hair, girt

round the waist with a strap; and he fed on bark and herbs.

He summoned the people to a change of life, in order to get rid of wickedness; and as a sign of the change of life, he bathed people in the Jordan. He said: "A voice calls to you: Open a way for God through the wild places, clear the way for Him. Make it so that all may be level, that there may be neither hollows nor hills, neither high nor low. Then God will be among you, and all will find their salvation." Mk. I. 4

Lk. III. 4

5

6

And the people asked him, "What are we to do?" He answered: "Let him who has two suits of clothes give one to him who has none. Let him who has food give to him who has none." And tax-collectors came to him, and asked: "What are we to do?" He said to them: "Extort nothing beyond what is ordered." And soldiers asked: "How are we to live?" He said: "Do no one any harm, do not deal falsely; be content with what is served out to you." 10

11

12

13

14

And inhabitants of Jerusalem came to him, and all the Jews in the neighborhood of the Jordan. And they acknowledged their wickedness Mt. III. 5

6

to him; and, in sign of the change of life, he bathed them in the Jordan.

Mt. III. 7 And many of the orthodox and conventional religionists also came to John, but secretly. He recognized them, and said: "You race of vipers! Have you, also, got wind of it, that you cannot escape the will of God? Then bethink yourselves,

8 and change your faith! And if you wish to change your faith, let it be seen by your fruits what you

10 have bethought yourselves. The ax is already laid to the tree. If the tree produces bad fruit, it will

11 be cut down and cast into the fire. In sign of your change I cleanse you in water; but, along with this bathing, you must be cleansed with the

12 spirit. The spirit will cleanse you, as a master cleanses his threshing-floor; when he gathers the wheat, but burns the chaff."

13 Jesus came from Galilee to the Jordan to be bathed by John; and he bathed, and heard John's preaching.

iv. 1 And from the Jordan he went into the wild

2 places, and there he strove in the spirit. Jesus passed forty days and nights in the desert, without food or drink.

And the voice of his flesh said to him: "If Lk. iv. 3 you were Son of the Almighty God, you might of your own will make loaves out of stones; but you cannot do this, therefore you are not Son of 4 God." But Jesus said to himself: "If I cannot make bread out of stones, this means that I am not Son of a God of the flesh, but Son of the God of the spirit. I am alive, not by bread, but by the spirit. And my spirit is able to disregard the flesh."

But hunger, nevertheless, tormented him; and the voice of the flesh again said to him: "If you live only by the spirit, and can disregard the flesh, then you can throw off the flesh, and your spirit will remain alive." And it seemed to him 9 that he was standing on the roof of the temple, and the voice of the flesh said to him: "If you are Son of the God of the spirit, throw yourself off the temple. You will not be killed. But an unfore- 10 seen force will keep you, support you, and save you from all harm." But Jesus said to himself: "I 11 can disregard the flesh, but may not throw it off, 12 because I was born by the spirit into the flesh. This was the will of the Father of my spirit, and I cannot oppose him."

Then the voice of the flesh said to him: "If you cannot oppose your Father by throwing yourself off the temple and discarding life, then you also cannot oppose your Father by hungering when you need to eat. You must not make light of the desires of the flesh; they were placed in you, and you must serve them." Then Jesus seemed to see all the kingdoms of the earth and all mankind, just as they live and labor for the flesh, expecting gain therefrom. And the voice of the flesh said to him: "Well, you see, these work for me, and I give them all they wish for. If you will work for me you will have the same." But Jesus said to himself: "My Father is not flesh, but spirit. I live by Him; I always know that He is in me. Him alone I honor, and for Him alone I work, expecting reward from Him alone."

Then the temptation ceased, and Jesus knew the power of the spirit.

And when he had known the power of the spirit, Jesus went out of the wild places, and went again to John, and stayed with him.

And when Jesus was leaving John, John

said of him: "This is the saviour of men."

On account of these words of John, two of John's disciples left their former teacher and went after Jesus. Jesus, seeing them following him, stopped and said: "What do you want?" They said to him: "Teacher! we wish to be with you, and to know your teaching." He said: "Come with me, and I will tell you everything." They went with him, and stayed with him, listening to him until the tenth hour. Jn. l. 37

One of these disciples was called Andrew. Andrew had a brother Simon. Having heard Jesus, Andrew went to his brother Simon, and said to him: "We have found him of whom the prophets wrote, the Messiah; we have found him who has announced to us our salvation." Andrew took Simon with him, and brought him also to Jesus. Jesus called this brother of Andrew, Peter, which means a stone. And both these brothers became disciples of Jesus.

Afterward, before entering Galilee, Jesus met Philip, and called him to go with him. Philip was from Bethsaida, and a fellow-villager of Peter and Andrew. When Philip knew Jesus, he went

and found his brother Nathanael, and said to him: "We have found the chosen of God, of whom the prophets and Moses wrote. This is Jesus, the son of Joseph, from Nazareth."
Jn. I. 46 Nathanael was astonished that he of whom the prophets wrote should be from the neighboring village, and said: "It is most unlikely that the 47 messenger of God should be from Nazareth." Philip said: "Come with me, you shall see and 48. hear for yourself." Nathanael agreed, and went with his brother, and met Jesus; and, when he 49 had heard him, he said to Jesus: "Yes, now I see that this is true, that you are the Son of God and 51 the king of Israel." Jesus said to him: "Learn something more important than that. Henceforth heaven is opened, and people may be in communion with the forces of heaven. Henceforth God will be no longer separate from men."

Lk. iv. 16 And Jesus came home to Nazareth; and on the Sabbath he went as usual into the 17 synagogue, and began to read. They gave him the book of the prophet Isaiah, and, unrolling it, he began to read. In the book was written:—

18 "The spirit of the Lord is in me. He has

chosen me to announce happiness to the unfortunate and the broken-hearted, to announce freedom to those who are bound, light to the blind, and salvation and rest to the weary. To announce [19] to all men the time of God's mercy."

He folded the book, gave it to the attendant, and sat down. And all waited to hear what [20] he should say. And he said: "This writing has now been fulfilled before your eyes."

# 2

## Which Art In Heaven

### God Is The Spirit In Man

*Therefore man must work, not for the flesh, but for the spirit.*

Mt. xil. 1
Mk. II. 23
Lk. vl. 1 IT HAPPENED ONCE THAT JESUS, with his disciples, went through a field on the Sabbath. His disciples were hungry, and on the way plucked ears of corn, bruised them in their hands, and ate the grain. But, according to the teaching of the orthodox, God had made an agreement with Moses, that all should observe the Sabbath, and do nothing on that day. According to this teaching of the orthodox, God commanded that he who worked on the Sabbath Mt. xil. 2 should be stoned to death. The orthodox saw that the disciples were bruising ears of corn on the Sabbath, and said: "It is not right to do so on the Sabbath. One must not work on the Sabbath,

---

and you are bruising ears of corn. God ordained the Sabbath, and commanded the breaking of it should be punished with death." Jesus heard this, and said: "If you understand what is the  Mt. xii. 7
meaning of God's words, 'I desire love, and not sacrifice,' you would not attach blame to that which is not blameworthy. Man is more impor-  8
tant than the Sabbath."

It happened another time, on a Sabbath,  Lk. xiii. 10
that when Jesus was teaching in the synagogue, a  11
sick woman came up to him and asked him to help her. And Jesus began to cure her. Then the  12-14
orthodox church-elder was angry with Jesus for this, and said to the people: "It is said in the law of God: There are six days in the week on which to work." But Jesus, in reply, asked the orthodox  xiv. 3
professors of the law: "Well, then, in your opinion, may not one help a man on the Sabbath?" And they did not know what to answer. Then Jesus  6
said: "Deceivers! Does not each of you untie his  5
beast from the manger and lead him to water on  Lk. xiii. 15
the Sabbath? And if his sheep falls into a well, any  Mt. xii. 11
one will run and drag it out, although even on the Sabbath. And a man is much better than a sheep.  12

But you say that one must not help a man. What,

Mk. III. 4 then in your opinion, must one do on the Sabbath, good or evil: save a soul or destroy it? Good must be done always, on the Sabbath too."

Jesus once saw a tax-gatherer receiving

Mt. ix. 9 taxes. The tax-gatherer was called Matthew. Jesus began to speak with him, and Matthew understood him, liked his teaching, and invited him to his house, and showed him hospitality. When Jesus came to Matthew, there came also

10 Matthew's friends, tax-gatherers and unbelievers, and Jesus did not disdain them, and sat down, he and his disciples. And the orthodox saw this,

11 and said to Jesus' disciples: "How is it that your teacher eats with tax-gatherers and unbelievers?" According to the teaching of the orthodox, God forbade communion with unbelievers. Jesus heard, and said: "He who is satisfied with his

12 health does not need a doctor, but he who is ill, does. Understand what is the meaning of God's

13 words: 'I desire love and not sacrifice.' I cannot teach a change of faith to those who consider themselves orthodox, but I teach those who consider themselves unbelievers."

There came to Jesus orthodox professors of the law from Jerusalem. And they saw that his disciples and Jesus himself ate bread with unwashed hands; and these orthodox began to condemn him for this, because they themselves strictly observed, according to church tradition, how plates and dishes should be washed, and would not eat unless they had been so washed. Also, they would eat nothing from the market unless they had washed it.

And the orthodox professors of the law asked him: "Why do you live not according to church tradition, but take and eat bread with unwashed hands?" And he answered them: "But in what way do you break God's commandment, following your church tradition? God said to you: 'Honor your father and mother.' But you have twisted it so that every one can say: 'I give to God what I used to give my parents.' And he who so says need not support his father and mother. Thus, then, you break God's commandment by church tradition. Deceivers! The prophet Isaiah spoke the truth about you: 'Because this people only fall down before me in words, and honor

Mt. xv. 1
Mk. vii. 1
Mt. xv. 2
Mk. vii. 2

3

4

5

Mt. xv. 3

Mk. vii. 10,11

12

13

Mt. xv. 7

8

me with their tongue, while their heart is far from me; and because their fear of me is only a human law which they have learnt by heart; therefore I will perform a wonderful, an extraordinary thing upon this people: The wisdom of its wise men shall be lost, and the reason of its thinkers shall be dimmed. Woe to them who take thought to hide their desires from the Eternal, and who do their deeds in darkness.' And so it is with you: You leave that which is important in the law, that which is God's commandment, and observe your human tradition as to the washing of cups!"

And Jesus called the people to him, and said: "Hearken all, and understand: There is nothing in the world that, entering a man, could defile him; but that which goes forth from him, this defiles a man. Let love and mercy be in your soul, and then all will be clean. Try to understand this."

And when he returned home, his disciples asked him: "What do these words mean?" And he said: "Do you also not understand this? Do you not understand that everything external, that

49

which is of the flesh, cannot defile a man? The reason is, it enters not his soul, but his body. It <sup></sup> Mk. vii. 19 enters the body, and afterward goes out from it. Only that can defile a man which goes out from 20 the man himself, from his soul. Because from the soul of man proceed evil, fornication, impuri- 21 ty, murder, theft, covetousness, wrath, deceit, insolence, envy, calumny, pride, and every kind of folly. All this evil is out of the soul of man and it alone can defile a man." 23

After this, the Passover came, and Jesus went to Jerusalem, and entered the temple. In Jn. ii. 13 the inclosure of the temple stood cattle, cows, bulls, rams; and there were cotes full of pigeons, 14 and money-changers behind their counters. All this was necessary in order to make offerings to God. The animals were slaughtered and offered in the temple. This was the method of prayer among the Jews, as taught by the orthodox professors of the law. Jesus went into the temple, twisted a whip, drove all the cattle out of the 15 inclosure, and set free all the doves. And he scattered all the money, and bade that none of this 16 should be brought into the temple. He said: "The Mt. xxi. 13

Mk. xi. 17
(Isa. lvi. 7
Jer. vii. 4, 11) prophet Isaiah said to you: The house of God is not the temple in Jerusalem, but the whole world of God's people. And the prophet Jeremiah also told you: Do not believe the falsehoods that here is the house of the Eternal. Do not believe this, but change your life; do not judge falsely; do not oppress the stranger, the widow, and the orphan; do not shed innocent blood, and do not come into the house of God, and say: Now we may quietly do foul deeds. Do not make my house a den of robbers."

18     And the Jews began to dispute, and said to him: "You say that our piety is wrong. By what 19 proofs will you show this?" And, turning to them, Jesus said: "Destroy this temple and I will in three days awaken a new, living temple." And the 20 Jews said: "But how will you at once make a new temple, when this was forty-six years in Mt. xii. 6 building?" And Jesus said to them: "I speak to you of that which is more important than the 7 temple. You would not say this if you understood the meaning of the words of the prophet: I, God, do not rejoice at your offerings, but rejoice at your love to each other, The living temple is the

whole world of men, when they love each other."

And then in Jerusalem many people believed in what he said. But he himself believed in nothing external, because he knew that everything is within man. He had no need that any one should give witness of man, because he knew that in man is the spirit. Jn. II. 23 24 25

And Jesus happened once to be passing through Samaria. He passed by the Samaritan village of Sychar, near the place which Jacob gave to his son Joseph. There was Jacob's well. Jesus was tired, and sat beside the well. His disciples went into the town to fetch bread. And a woman came from Sychar to draw water, and Jesus asked her to give him to drink. And she said to him: "How is it that you ask me to give you to drink? For you Jews have no intercourse with us Samaritans." Iv. 4 5 6 8 7 9

But he said to her: "If you knew me, and knew what I teach, you would not say this, and you would give me to drink, and I would give you the water of life. Whoever drinks of the water you have will thirst again. But whoever 10 13 14 shall drink of the water I have shall always be satisfied, and this water shall bring him ever-lasting life." The woman understood that he was speaking of things divine, and said to him: "I see that you are a prophet, and wish to teach me. But how are you to teach me divine things, when you are a Jew and I a Samaritan? Our people worship God upon this hill, but you Jews say that the house of God is only in Jerusalem. You cannot teach me divine things, because you have one belief, and we another." And Jesus said to her: "Believe me, woman, the time is already here, when people, to pray to the Father, will come neither to this hill nor to Jerusalem. The time has come when the real worshippers of God will worship the Heavenly Father in spirit and with works. Such are the worshippers the Father needs. God is a spirit, and He must be worshipped in the spirit and with works." The woman did not understand what he told her, and said: I have heard that the messenger of God will come, he whom they call the anointed. He will then declare everything." And Jesus said to her: "It is I, the same

*Margin notes: Jn. iv. 19, 20, 21, 23, 24, 25, 26*

who has spoken with you. Expect nothing more."

After this, Jesus came into the land of Judea, and there lived with his disciples, and taught. At that time John taught the people near Salim, and bathed them in the river Enon. For John was not yet put in prison. <sup></sup> Jn. III. 22

23

24

And a dispute arose between the disciples of John and the hearers of Jesus, as to which was better, John's cleansing in water or Jesus' teaching. And they came to John, and said to him: "You cleanse with water, but Jesus only teaches, and all go to him. What have you to say of him?" John said: "A man of himself can teach nothing, unless God teach him. Who speaks of the earth, is of the earth; but whosoever speaks of God, is from God. It is nowise possible to prove whether the words that are spoken are from God or not from God. God is a spirit; He cannot be measured, and He cannot be proved. He who shall understand the word of the spirit, by this very thing proves that he is of the spirit. The Father, loving His Son, has intrusted all to him. Whoever believes in the Son has life, and

25

26

27

31

32-34

35

36

whoever does not believe in the Son has not life. God is the spirit in man."

Lk. xi. 37 After this there came to Jesus one of the orthodox, and invited him to dinner. Jesus went 38 in and sat down at table. The host noticed that he did not wash before dinner, and wondered 39-41 thereat. And Jesus said to him: "You orthodox wash everything outside; but are you clean inside? Be well-disposed to men, and all will be clean."

vii. 37 And while he sat in the house of the orthodox, there came a woman of the town, who was an unbeliever. She had learnt that Jesus was in the house of the orthodox man, and she came 38 there too, bringing a bottle of scent. And she knelt at his feet, wept, and washed his feet with her tears, wiped them with her hair, and poured 39 scent over them. The orthodox man saw this, and thought to himself: "He is hardly a prophet. If he were really a prophet, he would know what kind of a woman it is that is washing his feet. He would know that this is a wrongdoer, and would 40 not allow her to touch him." Jesus guessed his thought, and, turning to him, said: "Shall I tell

you what I think?" The host assented. And Jesus 41
said: "Well, it is this. Two men held themselves
debtors to a certain man of property, one for five
hundred pence, the other for fifty. And neither Lk. vii. 42
the one nor the other had anything to pay with.
The creditor pardoned both. Now, in your opinion, which will love the creditor more, and show
him greater attention? And he said: "Of course, 43
he that owed more." Jesus pointed to the 44
woman, and said: "So it is with you and this
woman. You consider yourself orthodox, and
therefore a small debtor; she considers herself
an unbeliever, and therefore a great debtor. I
came to your house; you did not give me water
to wash my feet. She washed my feet with her
tears, and wiped them with her hair. You did not 45
kiss me, but she kissed my feet. You did not give 46
me oil to anoint my head, but she anoints my
feet with precious scent. He who rests in ortho- 47
doxy will not do works of love, but he who considers himself an unbeliever will do works of
love. And for works of love, all is forgiven." And 48-50
he said to her: "All your wickedness is forgiven
you." And Jesus said: "All depends upon what

each man considers himself. Whoever considers himself good will not be good; but whoever considers himself bad will become good."

Lk. xviii. 10 And Jesus said further: "Two men once came into a temple to pray; one orthodox, and 11 the other a tax-gatherer. The orthodox man prayed thus: 'I thank Thee, God, that I am not as other men, I am not a miser, nor a libertine; I am not a rogue, not such a worthless fellow as that 12 tax-gatherer. I fast twice weekly, and give away a 13 tithe of my property.' But the tax-gatherer stood afar off, and dared not look up at the sky, but merely beat his breast, and said: 'Lord, look 14 down upon me, worthless as I am.' Well, and this man was better than the orthodox, for the reason that whoever exalts himself shall be humbled, and whoever humbles himself shall be exalted."

v 33 After this, disciples of John came to Jesus, and said: "Why do we and the orthodox fast much, while your disciples do not fast? For, according to the law, God commanded people to 34 fast." And Jesus said to them: "While the bridegroom is at the wedding, no one grieves. Only

when the bridegroom is away, do people grieve.    35
Having life, one must not grieve. The external    Lk. v. 36
worship of God cannot be combined with works
of love. The old teaching of the external worship
of God cannot be combined with my teaching of
works of love to one's neighbor. To combine my
teaching with the old, is the same as to tear off a
shred from a new garment and sew it on an old
one. You will tear the new and not mend the old.
Either all my teaching must be accepted, or all
the old. And having once accepted my teaching,
it is impossible to keep the old teaching, of
purification, fasting, and the Sabbath. Just as    37
new wine cannot be poured into old skins, or the
old skins will burst and the wine run out. But    38
new wine must be poured into new skins, and
both the one and the other will remain whole."

# 3

# Hallowed Be Thy Name
## God's Kingdom

*The life of all men has proceeded from the spirit of the Father.*

Mt. xi. 2,3 AFTER THIS, JOHN'S DISCIPLES came to ask Jesus whether it was he of whom John spoke; whether he was revealing the kingdom of God, and renewing men by the spirit? Jesus answered and said: "Look, listen,—and tell John, whether the kingdom of God has begun, and whether people are being renewed by the spirit. Tell him of what kingdom of God I am preaching. It is said in the prophecies that, when the kingdom of God shall come, all men will be blessed. Well, tell him that my kingdom of God is such that the poor are blessed, and that every one who understands me becomes blessed."

And, having dismissed John's disciples,

# THE GOSPEL IN BRIEF

Jesus began to speak to the people as to the kingdom of God John announced. He said: "When you went to John in the wilderness to be baptized, what did you go to see? The orthodox teachers of the law also went, but did not understand that which John announced. And they thought him nothing worth. This breed of orthodox teachers of the law only consider that as truth which they themselves invent and hear from each other, and that as law which they themselves have divised. But that which John said, that which I say, they do not hearken to, and do not understand. Of that which John says, they have understood only that he fasts in the wild places, and they say: 'In him is an evil spirit.' Of that which I say, they have understood only that I do not fast, and they say: 'He eats and drinks with tax-gatherers and sinners—he is a friend of theirs.' They chatter with each other like children in the street, and wonder that no one listens to them. And their wisdom is seen by their works. If you went to John to look at a man attired in rich clothes, why, such dwell here in palaces. Then, what did you go to seek in the

Mt. xi. 16

18

19

17
19
8

9

desert? Did you go because you think John was the same as other prophets? Do not think this. John was not a prophet like others. He was greater than all prophets. They foretold that which might be. He has announced to men that which is, namely, that the kingdom of God was,

10 and is, on earth. Verily, I tell you, a man has not been born greater than John. He has declared

Lk. xvi. 16 the kingdom of God on earth, and therefore he is higher than all. The law and the prophets,—all this was needful before John. But, from John and to the present time, it is announced that the kingdom of God is on earth, and that he who makes an effort enters into it."

xvii. 20 And the orthodox came to Jesus, and began asking him: "How, then, and when, will the kingdom of God come?" And he answered them: "The kingdom of God which I preach is not such as former prophets preached. They said that God would come with divers visible signs, but I speak of a kingdom of God, the coming of which may not be seen with the eyes. And if any one shall say to you, 'See, it is come, or it shall come,' or, 'See, it is here or there,' do not believe them.

The kingdom of God is not in time, or in place, of any kind. It is like lightning, seen here, there, and everywhere. And it has neither time nor place, because the kingdom of God, the one which I preach, is within you." ²⁴ ²⁸

After this, an orthodox believer, one of the Jewish authorities, named Nicodemus, came to Jesus at night, and said: "You do not bid us keep the Sabbath, do not bid us observe cleanliness, do not bid us make offerings, nor fast; you would destroy the temple. You say of God, He is a spirit, and you say of the kingdom of God, that it is within us. Then, what kind of kingdom of God is this?"  Jn. III. 1,2

And Jesus answered him: "Understand that, if man is conceived from heaven, then in him there must be that which is of heaven."  ₃

Nicodemus did not understand this, and said: "How can a man, if he is conceived of the flesh of his father, and has grown old again enter the womb of his mother and be conceived anew?"

And Jesus answered him: "Understand what I say. I say that man, besides the flesh, is  ₅ also conceived of the spirit, and therefore every man is conceived of flesh and spirit, and therefore may the kingdom of heaven be in him. From flesh comes flesh. From flesh spirit cannot be born; spirit can come only from spirit. The spirit is that which lives in you, and lives in freedom and reason; it is that of which you know neither the beginning nor the end, and which every man feels in him. And, therefore, why do you wonder that I told you we must be conceived from heaven?"

Nicodemus said: "Still I do not believe that this can be so."

Then Jesus said to him: "What kind of a teacher are you, if you do not comprehend this? Understand that I am not interpreting some learned points; I am interpreting that which we all know, I am averring that which we all see. How will you believe in that which is in heaven if you do not believe in that which is on earth, which is in you yourself?

"For, no man has ever gone up to heaven, but there is only man on earth, come down from heaven, and himself of heaven. Now, this same heavenly Son in man it is that must be lifted up, Jn. III. 15 that every one may believe in him and not perish, but may have heavenly life. For God gave 16 His Son, of the same essence as Himself, not for men's destruction, but for their happiness. He gave him in order that every one might believe in him, and might not perish, but have life without 17 end. For He did not bring forth His Son, this life, into the world of men in order to destroy the world of men; but He brought forth His Son, this life, in order that the world of men might be made alive through him.

"Whoever commits his life to him does not 18 die; but he who does not commit his life to him destroys himself thereby, in that he has not trust- 19 ed to that which is life. Death consists in this, that life is come into the world, but men them- selves go away from life.

"Light is the life of men; light came into 20 the world, but men prefer the darkness to light, and do not go to the light. He who does wrong does not go to the light, so that his deeds may not be seen, and such a one bereaves himself of 21 life. Whereas he who lives in truth goes to the light, so that his deeds are seen; and he has life, and is united with God.

"The kingdom of God must be understood, not, as you think, in the sense that it will come for all men at some time or other, and in some place or other, but thus,—In the whole world always, some people, those who trust in the heavenly Son of man, become sons of the kingdom, but others who do not trust in him are destroyed. The Father of that spirit which is in man is the father of those only who acknowledge themselves to be His sons. And, therefore, only those exist to Him who have kept in themselves that which He gave them."

Mt. xIII. 3     And, after this, Jesus began to explain to the people what the kingdom of God is, and he made this clear by means of parables.

He said: "The Father,—who is spirit,— 4   sows in the world the life of understanding, as the husbandman sows seed in his field. He sows over the whole field, without remarking where any particular seed falls. Some seeds fall 5   upon the road, and the birds fly down and peck them up. And others fall among stones; and

although among these stones they come up,
they wither, because there is no room for the Mt. xiii. 7
roots. And others, again, fall among wormwood,
so that the wormwood chokes the corn, and the 8
ear springs up, but does not fill. And others fall
on good soil; they spring up, and make return
for the lost corn, and bear ears, and fill, and
one ear will give a hundredfold, another sixtyfold, and another thirtyfold. Thus, then, God
also sowed broadcast the spirit in men; in some
it is lost, but in others it yields a hundredfold:
these last are they who form the kingdom of Mk. iv. 26
God. Thus the kingdom is not such as you
think, that God will come to reign over you.
God has only sown the spirit, and the kingdom
of God will be in those who preserve it.

"God does not force men. It is as when the 27
sower casts the seeds in the earth, and himself
thinks no more of them; but the seeds of them- 28
selves swell, sprout up, put forth leaf, sheath,
and ear, and fill with grain. Only when it is 29
ripened, the master sends sickles to reap the
cornfield. So also God gave His Son, the spirit, to
the world; and the spirit of itself grows in the

world, and the sons of the spirit make up the kingdom of God.

Mt. xiii. 23 A woman puts yeast in the kneading trough and mixes it with the flour; she then stirs it no more, but lets it ferment and rise. As long as men live, God does not interpose in their life. He gave the spirit to the world, and the spirit itself lives in men, and men who live by the spirit make up the kingdom of God. For the spirit there is neither death nor evil. Death and evil are for the flesh, but not for the spirit.

24 The kingdom of God comes in this way. A farmer sowed good seed in his field. The farmer is the Spirit, the Father; the field is the world; the good seeds are the sons of the kingdom of 25 God. And the farmer lay down to sleep, and an enemy came and sowed darnel in the field. The 27 enemy is temptation; the darnel is the sons of temptation. And his laborers came to the farmer and said: "Can you have sown bad seed? Much 28 darnel has come up in your field. Send us, we 29 will weed it out." And the farmer said: "You must not do that, for in weeding the darnel you will trample the wheat. Let them grow together.

The harvest will come, when I shall bid the <sub>Mt. xiii. 30</sub> reapers take away the darnel and burn it; and the wheat I shall store in the barn."

Now, the harvest is the end of man's life, and the harvesters are the power of heaven. And the darnel shall be burnt, but the wheat shall be cleaned and gathered. Thus also, at life's end, all shall vanish which was a guile of time, and the true life in the spirit shall alone be left. For the Spirit, the Father, there is no evil. The spirit keeps that which it needs, and that which is not of it does not exist for it.

The kingdom of God is like a net. The net 47 will be spread in the sea, and will catch all kinds of fish. And afterward, when it is drawn out, the 48 worthless will be set aside and thrown into the sea. So will it be at the end of the age; the powers of heaven will take the good, and the evil will be cast away.

And when he finished speaking, the disci- 10 ples asked him how to understand these parables? And he said to them: "These parables must 11 be understood in two ways. I speak all these parables because there are some like you, my disciples, who understand wherein is the kingdom of God, who understand that the kingdom of God is within every man, who understand how to go into it; while others do not understand this. Others look, but see not; they hearken, and do not understand, because their heart has become gross. Therefore I speak these parables with two meanings, for both classes of hearers. To the others I speak of God, of what God's kingdom is to them, and they may understand this; while to you I speak of what the kingdom of God is for you—that kingdom which is within you.

"And see that you understand as you ought the parable of the sower. For you the parable is this: Every one who has understood the meaning of the kingdom of God, but has not accepted it in his heart, to him temptation comes and robs him of that which has been sown: this is the seed on the wayside. That which was sown on stones, is he who at once accepts with joy. But there is not root in him, and he only accepts for a time; but let straits and persecution befall him, because of the meaning of the kingdom, and he straightway denies it.

That which was sown among the wormwood is he who understood the meaning of the kingdom, but worldly cares and the seductions of wealth strangle the meaning in him, and he yields no <sub></sub> Mt. xiii. 23 fruit. But that which was sown on good soil is he who understood the meaning of the kingdom, and accepted it into his heart; such yield fruit, one a hundredfold, another sixtyfold, another 12 thirtyfold. For he who retains, to him much is given; while from him who does not retain, the whole will be taken.

"And, therefore, take care how you under- Lk. viii. 18 stand these parables. Understand them so as not to give way to deceit, wrong, and care; but so as to yield thirtyfold, or sixtyfold, or a hundredfold.

"The kingdom of heaven grows and Mt. xiii. 31 spreads in the soul out of nothing, providing everything. It is like a birch seed, the very smallest of seeds, which, when it grows up, becomes greater than all other trees, and the birds of heaven build their nests in it."

# 4

# Thy Kingdom Come
## May All Men Enter God's Kingdom

*The will of the Father is the life and welfare of all men.*

Mt. ix. 35 AND JESUS WENT AMONG the towns and
36 villages, and taught all men the happiness of fulfilling the Father's will. Jesus was sorry for men,
that they perish without knowing wherein is the
true life, and are driven about and suffer, without
knowing why, like sheep left without a shepherd.

v. 1 Once a crowd of people gathered to Jesus,
to hear his teaching; and he went up on a hill
and sat down. His disciples surrounded him.

2 And Jesus began to teach the people as to
what is the Father's will. He said:—

Lk. vi. 20,21 "Blessed are the poor and homeless, for
they are in the will of the Father. Even if they
hunger for a time, they shall be satisfied; and if

they grieve and weep, they shall be comforted. If <sub>Lk. vi. 22</sub> people look down upon them, and thrust them aside and everywhere drive them away, let them <sub>23</sub> be glad at this; for the people of God have ever been persecuted thus, and they receive a heavenly reward.

"But woe to the rich, for they have already <sub>24</sub> got everything they wish, and will get nothing more. They are now satisfied; but they shall be hungry. Now they are merry; but they shall be <sub>25,26</sub> sad. If all praise them, woe to them, because only deceivers get everybody's praise.

"Blessed are the poor and homeless, but blessed only then, when they are poor, not merely externally, but in spirit; as salt is good only when it is true salt; not externally only, but when it has the savor of salt.

"So, you also, the poor and homeless, are the teachers of the world; you are blessed, if you <sub>Mt. v. 13</sub> know that true happiness is in being homeless and poor. But if you are poor only externally, then you, like salt without savor, are good for nothing. You must be a light to the world; therefore do not hide your light, but show it to men. <sub>14</sub>

For when one lights a candle, one does not put it under a bench, but upon the table, that it may light all in the room. So, you also, do not hide your light, but show it by your works, so that men may see that you know the truth, and looking at your good works, may understand your Heavenly Father.

"And do not think that I free you from the law. I teach not release from the law, but I teach the fulfillment of the eternal law. As long as there are men under heaven, there is an everlasting law. There will be no law, only when men shall of themselves act wholly according to the eternal law. And now I am giving you the commandments of the eternal law. And if any one shall release himself, if only from one of these short commandments, and shall teach others that they may so release themselves, he shall be least in the kingdom of heaven; while he who shall fulfill them, and shall thereby teach others, shall be the greatest in the kingdom of heaven. Because if your virtue be not greater than the virtue of the orthodox leaders, you will in no way be in the kingdom of heaven."

*These are the commandments:—*

I

In the former law it was said: "Do not kill."  <sub>Mt. v. 21</sub>
But if any one shall kill another, he must be
judged.

But I tell you, that every one is worthy of  22
judgment who gets angry with his brother. And
still more to blame is he who abuses his brother.

So that, if you wish to pray to God, remem-  23
ber, first, whether there is no man who may have
something against you. If you remember that but
one man considers you have offended him, leave  24
your prayer, and go first and make peace with
your brother; and then you may pray. Know that
God wants neither sacrifice nor prayer, but
peace, concord, and love among you. And you
may neither pray, nor think of God, if there is but
one man to whom you do not bear love.

And so this is the first commandment: Do
not be angry, do not abuse; but having quarreled,

make peace in such a way that no one may have cause for offense against you.

## II

Mt. v. 31 In the former law it was said: "Do not commit adultery; and if you wish to put away your wife, give her a bill of divorce."

28 But I tell you, if you are drawn by the beauty of a woman, you are already committing adul-

29 tery. All sensuality destroys the soul, and therefore it is better for you to renounce the pleasure of the flesh than to destroy your life.

32 And if you put away your wife, then, besides being vicious yourself, you drive her also into vice, and him who shall have to do with her.

And therefore, this is the second commandment: Do not think that love toward woman is good; do not admire the beauty of women, but live with the one to whom you have become united, and do not leave her.

## III

In the former law it was said: "Do not utter the name of the Lord your God in vain, do not <sub>Mt. v. 33</sub> call upon your God when lying, and do not dishonor the name of your God. Do not swear by Me in untruth, so as to profane your God." But I tell you that every oath is a profanation of God.      34

Therefore, swear not at all. Man cannot promise anything, because he is wholly in the      35 power of the Father. A man cannot turn one hair from gray to black; how then shall he swear      36 beforehand, that he will do this and that, and swear by God? Every oath is a profanation of God, for, if a man shall have to fulfill an oath which is against the will of God it must follow that he has sworn to go against God's will; so that every oath is evil. But when men question      37 you about anything, say: "Yes," if yes,—"No," if no. Everything added to this is evil.

Therefore, the third commandment is: Swear nothing, to any one; say "Yes" when it is yes,—"No," when it is no; and understand that every oath is evil.

## IV

In the former law it was said: "He who destroys life, shall give a life for a life; and an eye for an eye, a tooth for a tooth, a hand for a hand, an ox for an ox, a slave for a slave," and so on.

But I tell you: Do not wrestle with evil by evil. Not only do not take by law an ox for an ox, a slave for a slave, a life for a life, but do not resist evil at all. If any one wishes to take an ox from you by law, give him another; if any one wishes to get your coat by law, give him your shirt also; if any one strikes out your tooth on one side, turn to him the other side. If you are made to do one piece of work, do two. If men wish to take your property, give it to them. If they do not return your money, do not ask for it.

And therefore: Do not judge, do not go to law, do not punish, and you yourself shall not be judged, nor punished. Forgive all, and you shall be forgiven, because if you shall judge people, they will judge you also.

You cannot judge, because you, all men, are blind, and do not see the truth. How, with obstructed eyes, will you discern the mote in your brother's eye? You must first clear your own eye. But whose eyes are clear? Can a blind man lead a blind man? Both will fall into the pit. Thus, also, they who judge and punish, like the blind, are leading the blind. Mt. vii. 1

3

Lk. vi. 38

They who judge and condemn people to violent treatment, wounds, maiming, death, wish to teach people. But what else can come from their teaching, than that the pupil will learn his lesson, and will become quite like the teacher? What, then, will he do, when he has learnt his lesson? The same that the teacher does: violence, murder. 40

And do not think to find justice in the courts. To seek legal justice, to hand matters over to human courts, is the same as to cast precious pearls before swine; they will trample upon it, and tear you to pieces. Mt. vii. 6

And, therefore, the fourth commandment is: However men may wrong you, do not resist evil, do not judge and do not go to law, do not complain and do not punish.

V

In the former law it was said: "Do good to men of your own nation, and do evil to strangers."

But I tell you, love not only your own countrymen, but people of other nations. Let strangers hate you, let them fall upon you, wrong you; but you speak well of them, and do them good. If you are only attached to your countrymen, why, all men are thus attached to their own countrymen, and hence wars arise. Behave equally well toward men of all nations, and you will be the sons of the Father. All men are His children, and therefore all are brothers to you.

And, therefore, this is the fifth commandment: Behave equally well toward foreigners, as I told you to behave among yourselves. Before the Father of all men there are neither different nations nor different kingdoms: all are brothers, all sons of one Father. Make no distinction among people as to nations and kingdoms.

And so: I. Do not be angry, but be at peace with all men. II. Do not seek delight in sexual gratification. III. Do not swear anything to any one. IV. Do not oppose evil, do not judge, and do not go to law. V. Do not make any distinction among men as to nationality, and love strangers like your own people.

All these commandments are contained in this one: All that you wish people should do for you, do you even so to them. <sub>Mt. vii. 12</sub>

Fulfill my teaching, not for men's praise. If you do it for men, then from men you have your reward. But if not for men, then your reward is from the Heavenly Father. So that, if you do good to men, do not boast about it before men. Thus hypocrites do, that men may speak well of them. And they get what they wish. But if you do good to men, do it so that no one may see it so that your left hand may not know what your right hand is doing. And your Father will see this, and will give you what you need.

And, if you wish to pray, do not pray like the hypocrites. Hypocrites love to pray in churches, in the sight of men. They do this for men's sake, and get in return from men that which they wish.

M. vi. 6 But, if you wish to pray, go where no one may see you, and pray to your Father, the Spirit, and the Father will see what is in your soul, and will give you that which you wish in the spirit.

7
8 When you pray, do not chatter with your tongue like the hypocrites. Your Father knows what you want before you open your lips.

Pray only thus:

M. vi. 9
*Our Father, without beginning and with-out end, like heaven!*
*May Thy being only be holy.*
10
*May power be only Thine, so that Thy will be done, without beginning and without end, on earth.*
*Give me food of life in the present.*
11
12
*Smooth out my former mistakes, and wipe them away; even as I so do with all the mistakes of my brothers, that I may not fall into temptation, and may*
13
*be saved from evil.*

---

*Because Thine is the power and might,
and Thine the judgment.*

If you pray, above all, bear no one any malice. For if you do not forgive men their wrongdoing, the Father also will not forgive you yours.

If you fast and go hungry, do not show it to men; thus do the hypocrites, that people may see, and speak well of them. And people speak well of them, and they get what they wish. But do not you do so; if you suffer want, go about with a cheerful face, that people may not see. But your Father will see, and will give you what you need.

Do not lay up store on earth. On earth, the worm consumes, and rust eats, and thieves steal. But lay up heavenly wealth for yourself. Heavenly wealth the worm does not gnaw, nor rust eat, nor thieves steal. Where your wealth is, there will your heart also be.

The light of the body is the eye, and the light of the soul is the heart. If your eye is dim, then all your body will be in darkness. And if the light of your heart is dim, then all your soul will

24 be in darkness. You cannot serve at one time
two masters. You will please one, and offend the
other. You cannot serve God and the flesh. You
will either work for the earthly life or for God.
25 Therefore, do not be anxious for what you shall
eat and drink, and wherewith you shall be
clothed. Life is more wonderful than food and
clothing, and God gave it to you.

Look at God's creatures, the birds. They
Mt. vi. 26 do not sow, reap, or harvest, but God feeds
them. In God's sight, man is not worse than the
bird. If God gave man life, He will be able to feed
him too. But you yourselves know that, however
27 much you strive, you can do nothing for yourselves. You cannot lengthen your life by an hour.
And why should you care about clothing? The
28 flowers of the field do not work and do not spin,
29 but are dressed as Solomon in all his glory never
30 was. Well, then, if God has so adorned the grass,
which today grows and tomorrow is mown, will
he not clothe you?

Do not trouble and worry yourselves; do
31 not say that you must think of what you will eat
and how you will be clothed. This every one

needs, and God knows this need of yours. And Mt. vi. 32
so, do not care about the future. Live in the present day. Take care to be in the will of the 33
Father. Wish for that which alone is important, and the rest will all come of itself. Strive only to be in the will of the Father. And so, do not trouble about the future. When the future comes, then it will be time to do so. There is enough evil in the present. 34

Ask and it shall be given you, seek and you shall find, knock and it shall be opened to you. Lk. xi. 9
Is there a father who would give his son a stone instead of bread, or a snake instead of fish? Mt. vii. 9,10
When, how is it that we, wicked men, are able to give our children that which they need, while 11
your Father in heaven shall not give you that which you truly need, if you ask Him? Ask, and the Heavenly Father will give the life of the spirit to them who ask Him.

The way to life is narrow, but enter by the narrow way. The way into life is one only. It is 13
narrow and straight. About it the plain lies great and wide, but it is the way of destruction. The narrow way alone leads to life; and few find it.

# Thy Kingdom Come

Mt. vii. 14
Lk. xii. 32 But do not quail, little flock! The Father has promised you the kingdom.

Mt. vii. 15 Only, beware of false prophets and teachers; they approach you in sheepskins, but within they are ravening wolves.

Mt. vii. 16
17
20
Lk. vi. 45 By their fruits will you know them; by that which they yield. Figs are not gathered from thistles, nor grapes from thorns. But a good tree brings forth good fruit. And a bad tree brings forth bad fruit. And so you will know them by the fruits of their teaching. A good man, from his good heart, brings forth everything that is good; but a wicked man, from his evil heart, brings forth everything evil; for the lips speak from the overflow of the heart. And therefore, if teachers teach you to do to others that which is bad for yourselves,—teach violence, executions, wars,—know that they are false teachers.

Mt. vii. 21
22 For it is not he that says: Lord, Lord! who shall enter the kingdom of heaven, but he who fulfills the word of the Heavenly Father. The false teachers will say: "Lord, Lord! we have taught your teaching, and we have driven away evil according to your teaching." But I will disown

them, and say to them: No, I never acknowledge Mt. vii. 23
you, and do not acknowledge you. Go out of my
sight, you are doing that which is unlawful.

And so, every one who has heard these
words of mine, and fulfills them, he, like a rea- 24
sonable man, builds his house upon a rock. And
his house will stand against all storms. But he 25
who hears these words of mine, and does not 26
fulfill them, he, like a foolish man, builds his
house upon sand. When the storm comes, it will
overthrow the house, and all will perish. 27

And all the people wondered at such
teaching; because the teaching of Jesus was Lk. iv. 32
quite other than that of the orthodox teachers of
the law. These taught a law which must be
obeyed, but Jesus taught that all men are free.
And in Jesus Christ were fulfilled the prophecies Mt. iv. 14
of Isaiah: "The people living in darkness, in the
shadow of death, saw the light of life, and he 16
who furnished this light of truth does no violence
nor harm to men, but he is meek and gentle. He,
in order to bring truth into the world, neither dis-
putes nor shouts; his voice is never heard raised. xii. 19
He will not break a straw, and will not blow out 20

the smallest light. And all the hope of men is in
<sup>Mt. xii. 21</sup> his teaching."

# 5

## THY WILL BE DONE

### Serving The Spirit Gives True Life

*The fulfillment of the personal will leads to death; the fulfillment of the Father's will gives true life.*

AND JESUS REJOICED at the strength of the Mt. xl. 25 spirit, and said:—

"I acknowledge the spirit of the Father, the source of everything in heaven and earth, Who has revealed that which was hidden from the wise and learned, to the simple, solely through their acknowledging themselves Sons of the Father.

"All take care for fleshly happiness, and 28 have put themselves to a load which they cannot draw; they have put a yoke upon themselves which was not made for them.

"Understand my teaching and follow it; and you shall know rest and joy in life. I give you another yoke, and another load; namely, the spir- 29 itual life. Put yourselves to that, and you shall learn from me peace and happiness. Be calm and meek in heart, and you will find blessedness in your life. Because my teaching is a yoke made for you, and the fulfillment of my teaching is a light load, with a yoke made for you."

The disciples of Jesus once asked him whether he wished to eat. He said: "I have food of which you do not know." They thought that some one had brought him something to eat. But he said:—

"My food is to do the will of Him who gave me life, and to fulfill that which He intrusted to me. Do not say 'There is still time,' as the plowman said, waiting for the harvest. He who fulfills the will of the Father is always satisfied, and knows neither hunger not thirst. The fulfillment of the will of God always satisfies, bearing its reward within itself. You must not say, 'I will afterward fulfill the will of the Father.' While there is life, you always can, and must, fulfill the will of the Father. Our life is the field which God has sown, and our business is to gather its fruits. And if we gather the fruits, we get the reward, life beyond time. True it is, that we do not give ourselves life; someone else does. And if we labor to gather in life, then we, like reapers, get our reward. I teach you to gather in this life, which the Father has given you."

Once, Jesus came to Jerusalem. And there Jn. v. 1,2 was then a bathing-place there. And men said of 4 this bathing-place, that an angel came down into it, and through this the water in the bath would begin to move, and he who first plunged into the water after it was moved got well from whatever he was ailing. And sheds were made around the 2 bath, and under these sheds sick men lay, wait- ing for the water in the bath to be moved, in 3 order to plunge into it.

And a man was there who had been infirm 5 thirty-eight years. Jesus asked who he was.

And the man told how he had been ailing so long, and was still waiting to get into the bath first, upon the water being moved, in order to be healed; but for these thirty-eight years he had been unable to get in first, others always getting into the bath before him.

And Jesus saw that he was old, and said to 6 him: "Do you wish to get well?"

He said: "I wish to, but I have no one to 7

carry me into the water in time. Some one always will get in before me."

Jn. v. 8 And Jesus said to him: "Awake, take up your bed and walk."

9 And the sick man took up his bed and walked.

10 And it was the Sabbath. And the orthodox said: "You must not take up the bed, for today is 11 the Sabbath." He said: "He who raised me, bade me also take up the bed." And the infirm man 15 said to the orthodox, that it was Jesus who had 16 healed him. And they became angry, and accused Jesus, because he did such things on the Sabbath.

17 And Jesus said: "That which the Father 19 always does, I also do. In truth, I say to you, the Son of himself can do nothing. He does only that which he has understood from the Father. What 20 the Father does, he also does. The Father loves the Son, and by this very fact has taught him everything which the Son should know.

21 "The Father gives life to the dead, and thus the Son gives life to him who desires it; because, as the business of the Father is life, so the busi-

ness of the Son must be life. The Father has not [22] condemned men to death, but has given men power, at will to die or live. And they will live, if [Jn. v. 23] they shall honor the Son as the Father.

"I tell you truly, that he who has under- [24] stood the meaning of my teaching, and has believed in the common Father of all men, already has life, and is delivered from death. They who have understood the meaning of [25] human life, have already escaped from death and shall live forever. Because, as the Father [26] lives of Himself, so also has He given the Son life [27] within himself. And He has given him freedom. It is by this, that he is the Son of Man.

"Henceforth all mortals shall be divided [28] into two kinds. They alone, who do good, shall [29] find life; but they who do evil shall be destroyed. And this is not my decision, but it is what I have [30] understood from the Father. And my decision is true, because I thus decide, not in order to do that which I wish, but in order that all may do that which the Father of all wishes.

"If I were to assure all that my teaching is [31] true, this would not establish my teaching. But

<sup>36</sup> there is that which establishes my teaching; namely, the conduct which I teach. That shows <sup>Jn. v. 37</sup> that I do not teach of myself, but in the name of the Father of all men. And my Father, He who has taught me, confirms the truth of my commandments in the souls of all.

<sup>38</sup> "But you do not wish to understand and to know His voice. And you do not accept the meaning this voice speaks. That that which is in you, is spirit descended from heaven,—this, you do not believe.

<sup>39</sup> "Enter into the meaning of your writings. You will find in them the same as in my teaching, commandments to live, not for yourself alone, <sup>40</sup> but for the good of men. Why, then, do you not wish to believe in my commandments, which are <sup>43</sup> those that give life to all men? I teach you in the name of the common Father of all men, and you do not accept my teaching; but if any one shall teach you in his own name, him will you believe.

<sup>44</sup> "One cannot believe that which people say to each other, but one can only believe that in every man there is a Son like the Father."

<sup>Lk. xix. 11</sup> And that men may not think that the king-

dom of heaven is established by anything visible; but that they may understand that the kingdom of God consists in the fulfillment of the Father's will; and understand that the fulfillment of the Father's will depends on each man's effort and striving to make people see that life is given, not for oneself personally, but for the fulfillment of the Father's will, which alone saves from death and gives life. Jesus told a parable. He said:— 12

"There was a rich man, who had to go away from his home. Before he went, he called 13 his slaves, and gave among them ten talents, one to each, and said: 'While I am away, labor each of you upon what I have given.' But it happened 14 that, when he was gone, certain inhabitants of 15 that town said: 'We do not wish to serve him any more.' When the rich man came back, he called the slaves to whom he had given the money, and bade each say what he had done with his money. 16 The first came, and said: 'See, master, for your one I have earned ten.' And the master said to 17 him: 'Well done, good servant; you have been trustworthy in a little, I will place you over much; be one with me in all my wealth.' Another slave

18 came, and said: 'See, master, for your talent I
Lk. xix. 19 have earned five.' And the master said to him:
20 'Well done, good slave, be one with me in all my
estate.' And yet another came, and said: 'Here is
your talent, I hid it in a cloth and buried I;
21 because I was afraid of you. You are a hard man,
you take where you did not store, and gather
22 where you did not sow.' And the master said to
him: 'Foolish slave! I will judge you by your own
words. You say that, from fear of me, you hid
your talent in the earth, and did not work upon
it. If you knew that I was severe, and take where
I did not give, then why did you not do that
. xxv. 26, 27 which I bade you do? If you had worked upon
Lk. xix. 23 my talent, the estate would have been added to,
and you would have fulfilled that which I bade
you. But you have not done that for which the
talent was given you, and, therefore, you must
24 not own it.' And the master bade the talent be
taken from him who had not worked upon it, and
25 given to him who had worked most. And then
the servants said to him: 'Sir, he already has
26 much.' But the master said: 'Give to them who
have worked much, because he who looks after

that which he has, shall receive an increase. As to them who did not wish to be in my power, <sub>Mt. xxv. 30</sub> drive them forth, so that they may be here no more."

Now this master is the source of life, the spirit, the Father. His slaves are men. The talents are the life of the spirit. As the master does not himself work upon his estate, but bids the slaves to work, each by himself, so the spirit of life in men has given them the command to work for the life of men, and then left them alone. They who say that they did not acknowledge the authority of the master, are they who do not acknowledge the spirit of life. The return of the master, and the demand for an account, is the destruction of fleshly life, and the decision of the fate of men as to whether they have yet life beyond that which was given them. Some, the slaves who fulfill the will of the master work upon that which was given them and make gain on gain; they are those men who, having received life, understand that life is the will of the Father, and is given to serve the life of others. The foolish and wicked slave, who hid his talent and did not work upon it, represents those men who fulfill only their own will, and not the will of the Father; who do not serve the life of others. The slaves who have fulfilled the master's will, and worked for the increase of his estate, become sharers of the whole estate of the master, while the slaves who have not fulfilled the master's will and have not worked for him, are bereft of that which was given them. People who have fulfilled the will of the Father, and have served life, become sharers in the life of the Father, and receive life, notwithstanding the destruction of the fleshly life. They who have not fulfilled the will, and have not served life, are bereft of that life which they had, and are destroyed. They who did not wish to acknowledge the authority of the master, such do not exist for the master; he drives them forth. People who do not acknowledge within themselves the life of the spirit, the life of the Son of Man, such do not exist for the Father.

Jn. vi. 1,2      After this, Jesus went into a desert place.
3     And many people followed him. And he climbed a mountain, and sat there with his followers. And

he saw that there was a great throng, and said: 5
"Whence shall we get bread to feed all these Jn. vi. 7
people?" Philip said: "Even two hundred pence
will not suffice, if to each be given but a little. We Mt. xiv. 17
have only a little bread and fish." And another Jn. vi. 9
disciple said: "They have bread; I have seen it.
There is a boy who has five loaves and two small
fishes." And Jesus said: "Bid them all lie down 10
on the grass."

And Jesus took the loaves which he had, 11
and gave them to his disciples, and bade them
give them to others; and so all began to hand
from one to another what there was, and all were
satisfied, yet much was left over.

The next day, the people came again to 26
Jesus. And he said to them: "See, you come to
me, not because you have seen wonders, but
because you have eaten bread and were
satisfied." And he said to them: "Work not for per- 27
ishable food, but for everlasting food, such as only
the spirit of the Son of Man gives, sealed by God."

The Jews said: "But what must we do, in 28
order to do the works of God?"

And Jesus said: "The work of God is in this, 29

to believe in that life which He has given you."

Jn. vi. 30 They said: "Give us a sign that we may believe. What are your deeds which can serve as 31 a proof? Our fathers ate manna in the wilderness. God gave them bread from heaven to eat; and so it is written."

32 Jesus answered them: "The true heavenly bread is the spirit of the Son of Man, that which 33 the Father gives. Because the nourishment of man is the spirit descended from heaven. This it 35 is which gives life to the world. My teaching gives true nourishment to man. He who follows me shall not hunger, and he who believes in my teaching will never know thirst."

36 "But I have already told you that you have seen this, yet do not believe.

37 "All that life which the Father gave the Son will be realized through my teaching; and every Jn. vi. 38 one who believes will be a sharer in it. I came down from heaven, not to do that which I wish, but to do the will of the Father, of Him who gave 39 me life. But the will of the Father who sent me is this, that I should keep all that life which He gave, and should not destroy anything of it. And

therefore, herein is the will of the Father who Jn. vi. 40 sent me, that every one who sees the Son, and believes in him, should have everlasting life. And my teaching gives life at the last day of the body."

The Jews were shocked at his saying that 41 his teaching was come down from heaven. 42 They said: "Why, this is Jesus, the son of Joseph; we know his father and mother. How, then, can he say that his teaching has descended from heaven?

"Do not debate as to who I am, and 43 whence I am come," said Jesus. "My teaching is 44 true, not because I declare, like Moses, that God spoke with me on Sinai; but it is true because it is in you also. Every one who believes my commandments, believes, not because it is I who speak, but because our common Father draws him to Himself; and my teaching will give him life at the last day. And it is written in the prophets, 45 that all shall be taught by God. Every one who shall understand the Father, and shall learn to understand His will, thereby yields himself to my teaching.

Jn. vi. 46 "That any man has seen the Father, this has never been, except he who is from God; he has seen, and sees, the Father.

47 "He who believes in me (in my teaching) has everlasting life.

48. 49 "My teaching is the nourishment of life. Your fathers ate manna, food straight from heav-50en, and yet they died. But the true nourishment of life, which descends from heaven, is such, 51 that he who is fed with it will not die. My teaching is this nourishment of life descended from heaven. He who is fed with it lives forever. And this nourishment which I teach is my flesh, which I give for the life of all men."

52 The Jews did not understand what he said, and began to dispute as to how it was possible to give one's flesh for the nourishment of men, and why.

53 And Jesus said to them: "If you shall not give up your flesh for the life of the spirit, there 54 will be no life in you. He who does not give up his flesh for the life of the spirit, has not real life. 55 That in me which gives up the flesh for the spirit, that alone lives.

"And therefore, our flesh is the true food for the real life. That only which in me consumes my body, that which gives up the fleshly life for the true life, that only is I. It is in me, and I am in it. And as I live in the flesh by the will of the Father, similarly, that which lives in me lives by my will." <sub>Jn. vi. 56</sub> <sub>57</sub>

And some of his disciples, when they heard this, said: "These are hard words, and it is difficult to understand them." <sub>60</sub>

And Jesus said to them: "Your ideas are so confused, that my sayings as to what man was, is, and always will be, seem difficult to you. Man is the spirit in the flesh, and the spirit alone gives life, but the flesh does not give life. In the words which seem so difficult to you, I have really said nothing more than that the spirit is life." <sub>61</sub> <sub>63</sub>

Afterward, Jesus chose seventy men out of his near friends, and sent them into those places where he himself wished to go. He said to them:— <sub>Lk. x. 1</sub> <sub>2</sub>

"Many people do not know the blessing of real life. I am sorry for all; and wish to teach all. But as the master is not enough for the reaping

of his field, so also I shall not suffice. Go you,
then, through the various cities, and everywhere
proclaim the fulfillment of the will of the Father.

Lk. x. 3

"Say, The will of the Father is in this: Not
to be angered, not to be sensual, not to swear,
not to resist evil, and not to make any distinction
between people. And accordingly, do ye in everything fulfill these commandments.

Mt. x. 16

"I send you like sheep among wolves. Be
wise as snakes, and pure as doves.

Lk. x. 4

"Before everything, have nothing of your
own; take nothing with you, neither wallet, nor
bread, nor money; only clothes upon your body,
and shoes. Further, make no distinction between
people; do not choose your hosts, where you
shall put up. But in whichever house you shall
come first, stay there. When you come into the
house, greet the master. If he welcome you, stay;
if not, go into another house.

5

Mt. x. 12

22

23

"For that which you shall say, they will hate
you, and fall upon, and persecute you. And when
they shall drive you out, go into another village;
and if they all drive you out of that, go yet into
another. They will persecute you as wolves hunt

sheep; but do not quail, suffer to the last hour. And they will take you into the courts, and will try you, and will flog you, and will take you before the authorities, that you may justify yourselves before them. And when you shall be taken into the courts, be not afraid; and do not bethink yourselves what you shall say. The spirit of the Father will speak through you, what is needful to be said. Mt. x. 19

"You will not have passed through all the towns, before people will have understood your teachings, and will turn to it. 23

"And so, be not afraid. That which is hidden in the souls of men will come forth. That which you shall say to two or three will spread among thousands. But chiefly, be not afraid of those who may kill your body. To your souls, they can do nothing. And so, do not fear them. But be afraid lest both your bodies and souls be destroyed, by your abstaining from the fulfillment of the will of the Father. That is what you have to fear. Five sparrows are sold for a farthing, but even they shall not die without the Father's will. And a hair shall not fall from the head without 27 26 28 29 30

Mt. x. 31  the Father's will. So then, what need you be afraid of, seeing you are in the Father's will?

"Not all will believe in my teaching. And they who will not believe, will hate it; because it bereaves them of that which they love, and strife will come of it. My teaching, like fire, will kindle the world. And from it strife must arise in the world. Strife will arise in every house. Father against son, mother against daughter; and their kin will become haters of them who understand my teaching, and they will be killed. Because, for him who shall understand my teaching, neither his father, nor his mother, nor wife, nor children, nor all his property, will have any weight."

Then the learned orthodox gathered at Jerusalem, and went to Jesus. Jesus was in a village, and a crowd of people thronged into the place, and stood around.

The orthodox began to speak to the people, in order that they might not believe in the teaching of Jesus. They said that Jesus was possessed; that if they should live by his commandments, there would then be yet more evil among the people than now. They said, that he drove out evil with evil.

Jesus called them to him, and said: "You say that I drive out evil with evil. But no power Mt. xii. 25 destroys itself. If it destroys itself, then it would 26 not be. You would drive out evil with threats, executions, murders; but evil, nevertheless, is 27 not destroyed, precisely because evil cannot make head against itself. But I drive out evil by other means than you do; that is to say, not with evil.

"I drive out evil by summoning people to fulfill the will of the Spirit, the Father, who gives 28 life to all. Five commandments express the will of the Spirit which gives happiness and life. And these commandments destroy evil. By their doing so, you have a proof that they are true. 29

"If men were not sons of one spirit, it would not be possible to overcome evil; as it is not possible to go into the house of a strong man, and rob it. In order to rob the house of a strong man, it is necessary first to bind the strong man. And men are bound thus in the unity of the spirit of life.

"And therefore I tell you, that every mis-

Mt. xII. 31 take of men, and every wrong interpretation, shall escape punishment; but false representation about the Holy Spirit, which gives life to all, shall not be forgiven to men. Should any one say 32 a word against man, that is not important; but should any one say a word against that which is holy in man, against the spirit, this cannot pass unpunished. Gird at me as much as you like, but do not call evil the commandments of life which I have disclosed to you. It cannot pass unpunished, if a man shall call that good which is evil.

"It is necessary to be at one with the spirit 30 of life. He who is not at one with it, is against it. It is necessary to serve the spirit of life and of good in all men, and not in oneself alone. You must either hold that life and happiness is good 33 for the whole world, then love life and happiness for all men, or else hold life and happiness an evil, and then not love life and happiness for yourself. You must either hold a tree good, and its fruit good or else hold a tree bad, and its fruit bad. Because a tree is valued by its fruit."

# 6

# On Earth, As In Heaven
## Man Must Forsake The Life Of The Flesh

*Therefore, in order to receive the true life, man must on earth resign
the false life of the flesh, and live by the spirit.*

AND THERE CAME once to Jesus his mother <sup></sup> Lk. viii. 19
and brothers, who could in no way get to see <sup></sup> Mt. xii. 46
him, because there was a great crowd around
him. And a man saw them, and went up to Jesus, <sup></sup> 47
and said: "Your family, your mother and brothers,
are standing without, and wish to see you."

And Jesus said: "My mother and my broth-
ers are they who have understood the will of the <sup></sup> Lk. viii. 21
Father, and fulfill it."

And a woman said: "Blessed is the womb
that has brought you forth, and the breasts that <sup></sup> xi. 27
you have sucked."

Jesus said to this: "Blessed only are they
who have understood the spirit of the Father, <sup></sup> 28

and keep it."

And a man said to Jesus: "I will follow you

Lk. ix. 57 whithersoever you may go."

And Jesus said to him, in answer: "You

58 cannot follow me; I have neither house nor place to live in. Wild beasts have their lairs and burrows, but man is everywhere at home, if he lives by the spirit."

And it happened once that Jesus was, with

Mk. iv. 35 his followers, sailing a boat. He said: "Let us pass over to the other side." A storm arose upon

37 the lake, and the boat began to fill, so that it nearly sank. And Jesus lay in the stern, and

38 slept. They woke him, and said: "Teacher, is it really all the same to you that we are perishing?" And, when the storm had fallen, he said: "Why

40 are you so timid? You do not believe in the life of the spirit."

Jesus said to a man: "Follow me."

Lk. ix. 59 And the man said: "I have an aged father, let me first bury him, and then I will follow you."

And Jesus said to him: "Let the dead bury

60 the dead, but to you, if you wish to truly live, fulfill the will of the Father, and make that will

known everywhere."

And again, another man said: "I wish to be your disciple, and will fulfill the will of the Father, <sub>Lk. ix. 61</sub> as you command, but let me first settle my family."

And Jesus said to him: "If the plowman look behind, he cannot plow. However strong the <sub>62</sub> reasons you have to look behind, so long as you look behind, you cannot plow. You must forget everything except the furrow you are driving; then only can you plow. If you consider as to what will be the outcome for the life of the body, then you have not understood the real life, and cannot live by it."

After this, it happened once that Jesus went with his disciples into a village. And a <sub>x. 38</sub> woman named Martha invited him into her house. Martha had a sister named Mary, who sat at the feet of Jesus, and listened to his teaching. <sub>39</sub> But Martha was busy getting ready the meal.

And Martha went up to Jesus, and said: <sub>40</sub> "Do you not see that my sister has left me alone to serve? Tell her to help me in the work."

And Jesus said to her in answer: "Martha,

Lk. x. 41 Martha! you trouble and busy yourself with many things, but only one thing is needful. And Mary has chosen that one thing which is needful, and 42 which none shall take from her. For true life the food of the spirit alone is needful."

And Jesus said to all: "Whoever wishes to Lk. 23 follow me, let him forsake his own will, and let him be ready for all hardships and sufferings of the flesh at every hour; then only can he follow 24 me. Because he who wishes to take heed for his fleshly life will destroy the true life. And he who fulfills the will of the Father, even if he destroy the fleshly life, shall save the true life. For, what 25 advantage is it to a man if he should gain the whole world, but destroy or harm his own life?"

And Jesus said: "Beware of wealth, xii. 15 because your life does not depend upon your having more than others.

"There was a rich man, who had a great 16 harvest of corn. And he thought to himself: Let me rebuild my barns. I will erect larger ones, and 17. 18 gather there all my wealth. And I will say to my 19 soul: 'There, my soul, you have everything after your desire; rest, eat, drink, and live for your pleasure.' But God said to him: 'Fool, this very Lk. xii. 20 night your soul shall be taken; and all that you have stored up shall go to others.'

"And thus it happens with every one who provides for the bodily life, and does not live in God."

21

And Jesus said to them: "Now, you say that Pilate killed the Galileans. But were these xii. 2 Galileans any worse than other people, that this happened to them? In no way. We are all such, 3 and we shall all perish likewise, unless we find salvation from death.

"Or of those eighteen men, whom the tower crushed in falling, were they particularly 4 worse than all the other dwellers in Jerusalem? In no wise. If we do not find salvation, sooner or later we shall perish in the same way. If we have 5 not yet perished as they, we must think of our 6 position, thus:—

"A man had an apple tree growing in his garden. The master came into the garden, and saw there was no fruit on the tree. And the master said to his gardener: 'It is now three years 7 since I have watched this apple tree, and it is still barren. It must be cut down, for as it is, it only spoils the place.' And the gardener answered: <sub>Lk. xiii. 8</sub> 'Let us wait yet a little, master; let me dig it round. I will dung it, and let us see what it will be next summer. Maybe it will yield fruit. But if it yields nothing by the summer, well then, we will cut it down.'

"Likewise we, as long as we live by the flesh, and yield no fruit to the life of the spirit, are barren apple trees. Only by the mercy of some power are we yet left for a summer. And if we do not yield fruit we shall also perish, even like him who built the barn, like the Galileans, like the eighteen men crushed by the tower, and like all who yield no fruit; perishing, dying forever, by death.

"In order to understand this, there is no need of special wisdom; each one sees this for himself. For not only in domestic affairs, but in that also which happens in the whole world, are we able to reason and to foresee. If the wind is in the west, we say there will be rain, and so it happens. But if the wind is from the south, we say there will be fair weather, and so it is. How,

then, is it that we are able to foresee the weath- Lk. xii. 56
er, and yet we cannot foresee that we shall all
die and perish, and that the only salvation for
us is in the life of the spirit, in the fulfillment of
its will?"

And a great multitude went with Jesus, and
he once more said to all:— xiv. 25

"He who wishes to be my disciple, let him
count for nothing father and mother, and wife 26
and children, and brothers and sisters, and all his
goods, and let him at every hour be ready for
anything. And only he who does as I do, only he
follows my teaching, and only he is saved from 27
death.

"Because every one, before beginning anything, will reckon whether that which he does is 28
profitable, and if it is profitable, will do it, but if
unprofitable, will abandon it. Every one who
builds a house will first sit down and reckon how
much money is wanted, how much he has, and
whether that will suffice to finish it. He will do this,
so that it may not happen that he should begin to 29
build, and not finish, for people will laugh at him.

"Likewise also, he who wishes to live the

Lk. xiv. 30 fleshly life must first reckon whether he can finish that with which he is busy.

"Every king, if he wishes to make war, will 31 first think whether he can go to war with ten thousand against twenty thousand. If he concludes 32 that he cannot, then he will send ambassadors, and make peace, and will not make war. So also, let every man, before giving himself over to the fleshly life, bethink him whether he can wage war against death, or whether death is stronger than he; and whether it is not then better for him to make peace beforehand.

"And so, each of you should first examine 33 what he considers his own family, money, or estate. And, when he has reckoned what all this avails him, and understands that it avails him nothing, then only can he be my disciple."

And upon hearing this, a man said: "That 15 is very well, if there be indeed a life of the spirit. But what if one abandons all, and there be no such life?"

To this Jesus said: "Not so; every one knows the life of the spirit. You all know it; but you do not do that which you know. Not because you doubt, but because you are drawn away from the true life by false cares, and excuse yourselves from it.

"This is like your conduct, like your deeds: A master got ready a dinner, and sent to invite guests, but the guests began to decline. One said: 'I have bought land, and I must go and look after it.' Another said: 'I have bought oxen, and I must try them.' A third said: 'I have taken a wife, and am going to celebrate the wedding.' And the messengers came and told the master that no one was coming. The master then sent the messengers to invite the beggars. The beggars did not refuse, but came. And when they were come, there was still room left. And the master sent to call in still more, and said: 'Go and persuade all to come to my dinner in order that I may have more people.' And they who had refused, from want of leisure, found no place at the dinner.

"All know that the fulfillment of the will of the Father gives life, but do not go because the guile of wealth draws them away.

"He who resigns false temporary wealth for the true life in the will of the Father, does as did

Lk. xvi. 1 a certain clever steward. There was a man who was steward to a rich master. This steward saw that, sooner or later, the master would drive him away, and that he would remain without food, 3 and without shelter. And the steward thought to himself: 'This is what I will do: I will privately distribute the master's goods to the laborers; I will reduce their debts, and then, if the master drives me out, the laborers will remember my kindness, and will not abandon me.' And so the steward 5 did. He called the laborers, his master's debtors, and rewrote their documents. For him who owed 6 a hundred he wrote fifty; for him who owed sixty, he wrote twenty, and similarly for the rest. And the master learned this, and said to himself: 8 'Well, he has done wisely; otherwise he would have had to beg his bread. To me he has caused a loss, but his own reckoning was wise.'

"For, in the fleshly life, we all understand wherein is the true reckoning, but in the life of the spirit, we do not wish to understand. This 9 must we do with unjust, false wealth,—give it up, in order to receive the life of the spirit. And if we Lk. xvi. 10 regret to give up such trifles as wealth for the life of the spirit, then this life will not be given us. If we do not give up false wealth, then our own true life will not be given us. <sup>11</sup>

"It is impossible to serve two masters at one time; to serve God and Wealth, the will of the Father, and one's own will. Either one or the other." <sup>12</sup>

And the orthodox heard this. But loving wealth, they jeered at him. <sup>14</sup>

And he said to them: "You think that, because men honor you on account of wealth, you are really honorable. It is not so. God does not look at the exterior, but looks at the heart. That which stands high among men, is abomination in the eyes of God. Now the kingdom of heaven is attainable on earth, and great are they who enter it. But they enter it, not the rich, but those who have nothing. And this has always been so, both according to your law, and according to Moses, and according to the prophets also. Listen: How does it stand with rich and poor in your way of thinking? <sup>15</sup> <sup>16</sup> <sup>17</sup>

"There was a rich man. He dressed well, led an idle and amusing life every day. And there <sup>19</sup>

Lk. xvi. 20 was a vagrant, Lazarus, covered with sores. And Lazarus came to the yard of the rich man, and

21 thought there would be leavings from the rich man's table, but Lazarus did not get even the leavings, the rich man's dogs ate up everything, and even licked Lazarus' sores. And both these

22 died, Lazarus and the rich man. And in Hades,

23 the rich man saw, far off, Abraham; and behold, Lazarus, the beggar, was sitting with him. And

24 the rich man said: 'Father Abraham, see, Lazarus the beggar is sitting with you. He used to wallow under my fence. I dare not trouble you, but send Lazarus the beggar to me, let him but wet his finger in water, to cool my throat, because I am burning in the fire.' But Abraham said: 'But why

25 should I send Lazarus into the fire to you? You, in that other world, had what you wished, but Lazarus only saw grief; so that he ought now to

26 be happy. Yes, and though I should like to help you, I cannot, because between us and you there is a great pit, and it is impossible to cross it. We are living, but you are dead.' Then the rich man

27 said: 'Well, Father Abraham, send Lazarus the beggar to my home. I have five brothers; I am

sorry for them. Let him tell everything to them, Lk. xvi. 28 and show how harmful wealth is; so that they may not fall into this torture.' But Abraham said: 'As it is, they know the harm. They were told of it 29 by Moses, and by all the prophets.' But the rich man said: 'Still, it would be better if some one should rise from the dead, and go to them; they 30 would the sooner bethink themselves.' But Abraham said: 'But if they do not listen to Moses 31 and the prophets, then, even if a dead man came to life, they would not listen, even to him.'

"That one should share all with one's brother, and do good to everybody; this all men know. And the whole law of Moses, and all the prophets, said only this: 'You know this truth, but cannot do it, because you love wealth.'"

And a rich official among the orthodox went up to Jesus, and said to him: "You are a good teacher, what shall I do to receive everlast- Mk. x. 17 ing life?"

Jesus said: "Why do you call me good? Only the Father is good. But, if you wish to have life, fulfill the commandments." 18

The official said: "There are many commandments; which do you mean?"

Mk. x. 19 And Jesus said: "Do not kill, Do not commit adultery, Do not lie, Do not steal. Further, honor your Father, and fulfill His will; and love your neighbor as yourself."

But the orthodox official said: "All these commandments I have fulfilled from my childhood; but I ask, what else must one do, according to your teaching?"

20

Jesus looked at him, at his rich dress, and smiled, and said: "One small thing you have left undone. You have not fulfilled that which you say. If you wish to fulfill these commandments: Do not kill, Do not commit adultery, Do not steal, Do not lie, and, above all, the commandment: Love your neighbour as yourself,—then, at once sell all your goods, and give them to the poor. Then you will have fulfilled the Father's will."

21

Having heard this, the official frowned, and went away, because he was loath to part with his estates.

And Jesus said to his disciples: "As you see, it is in no wise possible to be rich, and to fulfill the Father's will."

22

The disciples were horrified at these Mk. x. 23 words, so Jesus once more repeated them, and said: "Yes, children, he who has his own property, cannot be in the will of the Father. 24 Sooner may a camel pass through a needle's eye than he who trusts in wealth fulfill the will of the 25 Father." And they were still more horrified, and Lk. xviii. 25 said: "But, in that case, is it at all possible to keep one's life?"

He said: "To man it seems impossible to 26 support one's life without property; but God, even without property, can support a man's life."

Once, Jesus was going through the town of 27 Jericho. And in this town was the chief of the tax-gatherers, a rich man named Zaccheus. This Zaccheus had heard of the teaching of Jesus, xix. 1 and believed in it. And when he knew that Jesus 2 was in Jericho, he wished to see him. But there were so many people around, that it was impos- 3 sible to push through to him. Zaccheus was short of stature. So he ran ahead and climbed a tree, in order to see Jesus as he was going past. And thus, in passing by, Jesus saw him, and having 4 learned that he believed his teaching, said:

Jk. xix. 5 "Come down from the tree, and go home; I will come to your house." Zaccheus climbed down, ran home, made ready to meet Jesus, and joyfully welcomed him.

6 The people began to criticize, and to say of Jesus: "See, he has gone into the tax-gatherer's house,—the house of a rogue."

7 Meanwhile, Zaccheus said to Jesus: "See, sir, this is what I will do. I will give away half of my goods to the poor, and out of what is left I

8 will repay fourfold those whom I have wronged."

And Jesus said: "Now you have saved yourself. You were dead, and are alive; you were lost, and are found; because you have done as

9 Abraham did, when he wished to slay his son; you have shown your faith. Therein is the whole business of man's life; to seek out and save in his soul that which is perishing. But such sacri-

10 fice as yours must not be measured by its amount."

It happened once that Jesus and his disciples were sitting opposite a collecting box. People were placing their contributions in the

Mk. xii. 14 box, for God's service. Rich people went up to

the box, and put in much. And a poor woman, a widow, came and put in two farthings.

And Jesus pointed her out, and said: "See, now, this poor widow has put two farthings in the box. She has put in more than all. Because they put in that which they did not need for their own livelihood; while this woman has put all that she had; she has put in her whole life."

It happened that Jesus was in the house of Simon the leper. And a woman came into the house. And the woman had a vase of precious oil worth fifteen pounds. Jesus said to his disciples, that his death was near. The woman heard this, and pitied Jesus, and, to show him her love, wished to anoint his head with the oil. And she forgot everything, and broke the vase, and anointed his head and feet, and poured out all the oil.

And the disciples began to discuss among themselves, thinking that she had done wrong. And Judas, he who afterward betrayed Jesus, said: "See how much good stuff has gone for nothing. This oil might have been sold for fifteen pounds, with which, how many poor might have

been helped!" And the disciples began blaming
Mt. xxvi. 9 the woman; who was troubled, and did not know
whether she had done well or ill.

Then Jesus said: "You are troubling the
woman without cause. She has, indeed, done a
good work, and you mistakenly think of the poor.
10 If you wish to do good to the poor, do so; they
are always with you. But why call them to mind
now? If you pity the poor, go with your pity, do
11 them good. But she has pitied me, and done real
good, because she has given away all that she
had. Who of you can know what is useful, and
what is not necessary? How do you know that
there was no need to pour the oil over me? She
has thus anointed me with oil, and if it were but
to get ready my body for burial, this was needful.
She truly fulfilled the will of the Father, in forget-
ting herself and pitying another. She forgot the
reckonings of the flesh and gave away all that
13 she had."

And Jesus said: "My teaching is the fulfillment of the Father's will; and the Father's will
can be fulfilled by deeds only; not by mere
words. If a man's son, in answer to his father's

bidding, keeps saying, 'I obey, I obey,' but does nothing which his father bids, he then does not fulfill the will of his father. But if another son Mt. xxi. 28 keeps saying, 'I do not wish to obey,' and then goes and does his father's bidding, he indeed fulfills the father's will. And so with men: Not he is 29 in the Father's will who says: 'I am in the Father's will,'—but he who does that which the Father wishes."

# 7

## Give Us Our Daily Bread
### The Present Life Is Food For The True Life

*The true food of everlasting life is the fulfillment of the Father's will.*

Jn. vii. 1 AFTER THIS THE JEWS tried to condemn Jesus to death, and Jesus went away into Galilee, and lived with his relations.

The Jewish feast of tabernacles was come. And the brothers of Jesus got ready to go to the feast, and invited him to go with them. They did not believe in his teaching, and said to him:—

"Now, you say that the Jewish service of God is wrong, that you know the real service of God by deeds. If you really think that no one but yourself knows the true service of God, then come with us to the feast. Many people will be there, and you can declare before them all that the teaching of Moses is wrong. If all believe you, then it will be clear to your disciples also, that you are right. Why make a secret of it? You say Jn. vii. 4 that our service is wrong, that you know the true service of God; well then, show it to all."

And Jesus said: "For you, there is a special 6 time and place in which to serve God; but for me, there is none. I always and everywhere work for God. This is just what I show to people. I 7 show to them that their service of God is wrong, and therefore do they hate me. Go you to the 8 feast, and I will go when I think fit."

And the brothers went, but he remained 9, 10 behind, and only came up at the middle of the feast. And the Jews were shocked at his not honoring their feast, and delaying to come. And they discussed his teaching much. Some said that he 12 spoke the truth, while others said that he only disturbed the people.

At the middle of the feast, Jesus entered 14 the temple, and began to teach the people that their service of God was wrong; that God should be served not in the temple and by sacrifices, but in the spirit, and by deeds. All listened to 15 him and wondered that he knew the whole of wisdom without having learnt. And Jesus, having heard that all wondered at his wisdom, said to them:—

"My teaching is not my own, but His who sent me. If any one wishes to fulfill the will of the Spirit which sent us into life, he will know that I have not invented this teaching, but that it is of God. Because he who invents from himself, follows his own mere imaginations; but he who seeks the mind of Him who sent him, he is right, and there is no wrong in him.

"Your law of Moses is not the Father's law, and, therefore, they who follow it do not fulfill the Father's law, but work evil and falsehood. I teach you the fulfillment of the will of the Father alone, and in my teaching there cannot be contradiction. But your written law of Moses is all full of contradictions. Do not judge by outside appearance, but judge by the spirit."

And some said: "While he has been called a false prophet, see, he condemns the law, and no one makes a charge against him. Maybe in very deed he is a true prophet; maybe even the authorities have acknowledged him. Only one reason makes it impossible to believe him, namely, that it is said, when he who is sent from God shall come, no one will know whence he is come; but we know this man's birth and all his family."

The people still did not understand his teaching, and still sought proofs.

Then Jesus said to them: "You know me, and whence I am, after the flesh. But you do not know whence I am, after the spirit. You do not know Him, from whom I am according to the spirit; and that is the only needful knowledge. If I had said that I am Christ you would have believed me, the Man, but you would not have believed the Father who is in me, and in you. But it is necessary to believe the Father only.

"I am here among you for the short space of my life. I point out to you the way to that source of life, from which I have come forth. And you ask of me proofs, and wish to condemn me. If you do not know the way, then, when I shall be no more, you will in nowise find it. You must not discuss me, but must follow me. Whoever shall do that which I say, he shall know whether what I

Jn. vi. 28

29

33

34

say is true. He for whom the fleshly life has not become the food of the spirit, he who follows not the truth, thirsting for it as for water, cannot understand me. But he who thirsts for the truth, let him come to me to drink. And he who shall believe in my teaching shall receive the true life. He shall receive the life of the spirit."

And many believed in his teaching, and said: "That which he says is the truth and is of God." Others did not understand him, and still sought in prophecies for proofs that he was sent from God. And many disputed with him, but none could controvert him. The learned orthodox sent their assistants to contend with him, but their assistants returned to the orthodox priests and said: "We can do nothing with him."

And the high priests said to them: "But why have you not convicted him?" And they answered: "Never did any man speak as he."

Then the orthodox said: "It signifies nothing that it is impossible to controvert him, and that the people believe in his teaching. We do not believe, and none of the authorities believe. But the people is cursed, they were always stupid and unlearned; they believe every one."

And Nicodemus, the man to whom Jesus Jn. vii. 50 explained his teaching, said to the high priests: "It is impossible to condemn a man without hav- 51 ing heard him to the end, without understanding whither he is leading." But they said to him: "It is 52 useless to discuss, or pay any attention to this affair. We know that a prophet cannot come from Galilee."

At another time, Jesus was speaking with viii. 12 the orthodox, and said to them: "There can be no proofs of the truth of my teaching, as there cannot be of the illumination of light. My teaching is the real light, by which people tell what is good and what is bad, and therefore it is impossible to prove my teaching; which itself proves everything. Whoever shall follow me shall not be in darkness, but shall have life. Life and enlightenment, which are one and the same."

But the orthodox said: "You alone say 13 this."

And he answered them and said: "And if I 14 alone say this, yet I am right; because I know

whence I came, and whither I go. According to
my teaching, there is reason in life; whereas,
according to yours, there is none. Besides this,
not I alone teach, but my Father, the Spirit,
teaches the same."

They said: "Where is your Father?"

He said: "You do not understand my teaching, and therefore you do not know my Father.
You do not know whence you are and whither
you go. I lead you, but you, instead of following
me, discuss who I am. Therefore you cannot
come to that salvation of life to which I lead you.
And you will perish, if you remain in this error,
and do not follow me."

And the Jews asked: "Who are you?"

He said: "From the very beginning, I tell
you, I am the Son of Man, acknowledging the
Spirit as my Father. That which I have understood of the Father, the same I tell to the world.
And when you shall exalt in yourselves the Son
of Man, then you shall know what I am; because
I do and speak, not of myself, as a man, but I do
and speak that which the Father has taught me.
This I say, this I teach.

"And he who sent me is always with me; <sup>29</sup> and the Father has not left me, because I do His will. Whoever will keep to my understanding of <sub>Jn. viii. 31</sub> life, whoever will fulfill the will of the Father, he will be truly taught by me. In order to know the truth, it is necessary to do good to men. He who does evil to men, loves darkness, and goes into it; he who does good to men, goes to the light; so that, in order to understand my teaching, it is necessary to do good deeds. He who shall do <sup>32</sup> good, shall know the truth; he shall be free from evil and death. Because every one who errs <sup>34</sup> becomes the slave of his error.

"And as the slave does not always live in <sup>35</sup> the house of the master, while the son of the master is always in the house, so also a man, if he errs in his life and becomes a slave through his errors, does not live always, but dies. Only he who is in the truth remains always living. The truth is in this, to be not a slave, but a son. So that, if you err, you will be slaves and die. But if <sup>36</sup> you are in the truth, then you shall be free sons, and shall be living.

"You say of yourselves that you are sons of <sup>37</sup>

Abraham, that you know the truth. But see, you wish to kill me, because you do not understand Jn. viii. 38 my teaching. It comes to this, that I speak that which I have understood from my Father, and you wish to do that which you have understood from your father."

39      They said: "Our father is Abraham."

Jesus said to them: "If you were the sons 40 of Abraham you would do his deeds. But see, you wish to kill me because I told you that which I had learnt from God. Abraham did not do in that way; therefore you do not serve God, but serve your father, another one."

41      They said to him: "We are not bastards, but we are all children of our Father, all sons of God."

42      And Jesus said to them: "If your father were one with me, you would love me, because I 43 came forth from that Father. For I was not born of myself. You are not children of the one Father with me, therefore you do not understand my word; my understanding of life does not find place in you. If I am of the Father, and you of the same Father, then you cannot wish to kill me.

But if you wish to kill me, then we are not of one Father.

"I am from the Father of good, from God; Jn. viii. 44 but you are from the devil, from the father of evil. You wish to do the lusts of your father the devil, who is always a murderer, and a liar, with no truth in him. If he, the devil, says anything, he says what is of himself, and not common to all, and he is the father of lying. Therefore you are the servants of the devil and his children. Now 46 you see how plainly you are convicted of error. If I err, then convict me; but if there is no error in me, then why do you not believe in me?"

And the Jews began to revile him, and to 48 say he was possessed.

He said: "I am not possessed; but I honor 49 the Father, and you wish to kill me; therefore you are not brothers of mine, but children of another father. It is not I that affirm that I am right, but 50 the truth speaks for me. Therefore I repeat to 51 you: he who shall comprehend my teaching and perform it, shall not see death."

And the Jews said: "Well, do not we speak 52 the truth in saying that you are a Samaritan possessed, and that you convict yourself? The prophets died, Abraham died; but you say that he who performs your teaching shall not see death. Abraham died, and shall you not die? Or are you greater than Abraham?"

The Jews were still discussing as to whether he, Jesus of Galilee, was an important prophet, or unimportant, and forgot that he had told them that he said nothing of himself as a man, but spoke of the spirit that was within him.

And Jesus said: "I do not make myself to be anything. If I spoke of myself, of that which only seems to me, then all that I should say would mean nothing. But there is that source of everything which you call God; well, it is of Him that I speak. But you have not known, and do not know the true God. But I know Him, and I cannot say that I do not know Him; I should be a liar like you, if I said that I do not know Him. I know Him, and know His will, and fulfill it. Abraham, your father, saw and rejoiced over my understanding."

The Jews said: "You are only thirty years old, how were you living at the same time as

Abraham?"

He said: "Before Abraham was, there was Jn. viii. 58
the understanding of good, there was that which
I tell you."

Then the Jews picked up stones in order 59
to kill him, but he went away from them.

Jesus said: "My teaching is the awakening Jn. xi. 25
of life. He who believes in my teaching, notwithstanding that he dies in the flesh, remains living,
and every one who lives and believes in me shall 26
not die."

And yet a third time Jesus taught the peo- x. 1
ple; he said: "Men surrender themselves to my
teaching, not because I myself prove it. It is
impossible to prove the truth. The truth itself
proves all the rest. But men surrender to my
teaching, because there is no other than it; it is
known to men, and promises life.

"My teaching is to men as the shepherd's 2,3
familiar voice is to the sheep, when he comes
among them through the door, and gathers them,
to lead them to the pasture. But your teaching, 5
no one believes; because it is foreign to them,
and because they see in it your own lusts. It is

with men as with sheep, at the sight of a man who does not enter by the door, but climbs over the fence. The sheep do not know him, but feel that he is a robber. My teaching is the only true teaching; like the one door for the sheep. All your teachings of the law of Moses are lies, they are all like thieves and robbers to the sheep. He who shall give himself up to my teaching shall find true life; just as the sheep go forth and find food, if they follow the shepherd.

"A thief only comes to steal, rob, and destroy, but the shepherd comes to give life. And my teaching alone promises, and gives the true life.

"There are shepherds to whom the sheep are the chief interest in life, and who give up their lives for the sheep. These are true shepherds. And there are hirelings who do not care about the sheep, because they are hirelings, and the sheep are not theirs; so that if a wolf comes they abandon their charge and flee from them, and the wolf devours the sheep. These are false shepherds. And so there are false teachers, such as have no concern with the life of people; while true teachers give up their lives for the life of men.

"I am such a teacher. My teaching is this,—   Jn. x. 14,17 to give up one's life for the life of men. No one shall take my life from me, but I myself freely   18 give it up for men, in order to receive true life. The commandment to do this I received from my   15 Father. And as my Father knows me, so I also know Him; and therefore I lay down my life for   17 men. Therefore the Father loves me, because I fulfill His commandments.

"And all men, not only those here now, but   16 all men, shall understand my voice; and all shall come together into one, and all men shall be one, and their teaching one."

And the Jews surrounded him, and said:   24 "All that you say is difficult to understand, and does not agree with our writings. Do not torment us, but simply and straightforwardly tell us, whether you are that Messiah who, according to our writings, should come into the world."

And Jesus answered them: "I have already   25 told you who I am, but you do not believe. If you do not believe my word, then believe my works;

by them understand who I am, and wherefore I am come.

Jn. x. 26 "But you do not believe me because you

27 do not follow me. He who follows me, and does

28 that which I say, he understands me. And he who understands my teaching and fulfills it,

29 receives the true life. My Father has united them

30 with me, and no one can disunite us. I and the Father are one."

31 And the Jews were offended at this, and took up stones to kill him.

32 But he said to them: "I have shown you many good works, and have disclosed the teaching of my Father. For which, then, of these good works do you wish to stone me?"

33 They said: "Not for the good do we wish to stone you; but because you, a man, make yourself God."

34 And Jesus answered them: "Why, this is just what is written in your writings, where it says

35 that God Himself said to the wicked rulers: 'You

36 are gods.' If He called even vicious men gods, then why do you consider it sacrilege to call that the son of God, which God in His love sent into

the world? Every man in the spirit is the son of   37
God. If I do not live in God's way, then do not
believe that I am a son of God. But if I live after   Jn. x. 38
God's way, then believe from my life that I am in
the Father, and then you will understand that the
Father is in me and I in Him."

And the Jews began to dispute. Some said   20
that he was possessed, and others said: "A man   21
who is possessed cannot enlighten men." And
they did not know what to do with him, and   39
could not condemn him. And he went again   40
across the Jordan, and remained there. And
many believed in his teaching, and said that it   41
was true, as the teaching of John was. Therefore   42
many believed in it.

And Jesus once said to his disciples. "Tell   Mt. xvi. 13
me how the people understand my teaching
about the son of God and the son of man."

They said: "Some understand it like the   14
teaching of John, others like the prophecies of
Isaiah; others, again, say that it is like the teaching of Jeremiah. They understand that you are a
prophet."

"And how do you understand my teaching?"   15

And Simon Peter said to him: "In my opinion, your teaching consists in this, that you are the chosen Son of the God of Life. You teach that God is the life in man."

17  And Jesus said to him: "Happy are you, Simon, that you have understood this. No man could disclose this to you; but you have understood this, because God in you has disclosed it to you. Not fleshly understanding, and not I, my words, have disclosed this to you; but God my Father has directly disclosed it. And upon this is founded that society of men for whom there is no death."

# 8

# This Day
## Life Is Not Temporal

*Therefore true life is to be lived in the present.*

JESUS SAID: "He who is not ready for all flesh-  Mt. x. 38
ly sufferings and bereavements, has not understood me. He who shall obtain all that is best for  39.
the fleshly life, shall destroy the true life; he who
shall destroy his fleshly life in fulfilling my teaching, shall receive the true life."

And in answer to these words, Peter said to  xix. 27
him: "See, we have listened to you, have thrown
off all cares and property, and have followed
you. What reward shall we have for this?"

And Jesus said to him: "Every one who has  Mk. x. 29, 30
abandoned home, sisters, brothers, father, mother, wife, children, and his fields, for my teaching,
shall receive a hundredfold more than sisters
and brothers and fields, and all that is needful in

144

this life; and besides this, he receives life beyond the power of time. There are no rewards in the kingdom of heaven, the kingdom of heaven is its own aim and reward. In the kingdom of God all are equal, there is neither first nor last.

"Because the kingdom of heaven is like this. The master of a house went in the early morning to hire laborers for his grounds. He hired laborers at a penny a day, and set them to work in the garden. And he again went at mid-day and hired more, and sent them into the garden to work; and at evening he hired still more, and sent them to work. And with them all he agreed at a penny. The time came for the reckoning. And the master ordered all to be paid alike. First, those who came last; and afterward, the first. And the first saw that the last received each a penny. And they thought that they would receive more; but the first were also given each a penny. They took it and said: 'But how is this? They only worked one shift and we all four; why, then, do we receive alike? This is unjust.' But the master came up, and said: 'What are you complaining about? Have I offended you? The amount I hired

you for, I have given you. Our agreement was for  Mt. xx. 14
a penny, take it and go. If I wish to give to the last
the same as to you, am I not master of my own
will? Or because you see that I am good, is that  15
the cause of your grudging?'"

In the kingdom of God there is neither first
nor last, for all there are as one.  16

There came to Jesus two of his disciples,
James and John, and said: "Promise us that you  20
will do that for us which we shall ask of you."  Mk. x. 35

He said: "What do you wish?"

They said: "That we may be equal with  Mt. xx. 21
you."

Jesus said to them: "You yourselves do not
know what you ask. You may live just as I do,  22
and be cleansed from fleshly life like me, but to
make you like myself is not in my power. Every
man may, by his own effort, enter the kingdom of  23
his Father, having submitted to His power, and
fulfilling His will."

When they heard of this, the other disciples grew angry with the two brothers, because  24
these wished to be equal to their teacher, and
the first among his disciples.

But Jesus called them, and said: "If you

Mt. xx. 25 brothers, James and John, asked me to make you such as I am in order to be first among my disciples, then you were mistaken; but if you, my other disciples, are angry with them because they wish to be your elders, then you also are mistaken. Only in the world are kings and officials reckoned by seniority for governing the people. But among you, there cannot be either

26 elder or younger. Among you, for one to be greater than another, it is necessary to be the servant of all. Among you, let him who wishes to

27 be first, consider himself last. Because therein is

28 the will of the Father as to the Son of Man; who does not live to be served, but to himself serve all, and to give up his fleshly life, as a ransom for the life of the spirit."

And Jesus said to the people: "The Father

xviii. 11 seeks to save that which perishes. He rejoices

18 over it, as a shepherd rejoices when he has found one sheep that was lost. When one is lost, he leaves the ninetynine, and goes to save the lost one. And if a woman lose a farthing, she will

Lk. xv. 8 sweep out the whole hut and seek until she finds

it. The Father loves the Son, and calls him to Lk. xv. 10 Himself."

And he told them yet another parable, to the effect that they who live in the will of God xiv. 8 ought not to exalt themselves. He said: "If you are invited to dinner, do not seat yourself in the front corner; some one will come of more consideration than yourself, and the master will say: 'Leave your place, and allow him who is better than you to be seated. Then you will be put to 9 shame. But do better, take your seat in the very last place, then the master will find you, and call 10 you to a place of honor, and you will be honored.

"So also in the kingdom of God there is no 11 room for pride. He who exalts himself, by so doing lowers himself; but he who humbles himself, and considers himself unworthy, by this same means raises himself in the kingdom of God.

"A man had two sons. And the younger xv. 11 said to his father: 'Father, give me my property.' 12 And the father gave him his share. The younger 13 son took his share, went abroad, squandered all his property, and began to suffer want. And abroad, he became a swineherd. And he so hungered, that he ate acorns with the swine. And he bethought himself of his life, and said: 'Why did I take my share and leave my father? My father had plenty of everything; at my father's, even laborers ate their fill. But I here am eating the same food as the swine. I will go to my father, fall at his feet, and say: I am to blame, father, before you, and am not worthy to be your son. Take me back even as a laborer.' So he thought, and he went to his father. And when he was still far off, his father at once recognized him, and himself ran to meet him, embraced him, and began to kiss him. And the son said: 'Father, I am to blame before you, I am not worthy to be your son.' But the father would not even listen, and said to the laborers: 'Bring quickly the best clothes and the best boots, to clothe him and shoe him. And go and bring a fatted calf and kill it, and we will rejoice that this my son was dead and is now alive, was lost and is now found.' And the elder brother came from the field, and as he approached he heard the sounds of music in the

house. He called a servant to him, and said:
'Why is there this merry-making here?' And the
boy said: 'Have you not heard that your brother         Lk. xv. 27
is returned, and your father is full of joy, and has
ordered a fatted calf to be killed, for joy that his
son has returned?' The elder brother was offend-         28
ed, and did not go into the house. And the father
came out and called him. And he said to his         29
father: 'See, father, how many years I have
worked for you, and have not disobeyed your
command, while you never killed a fatted calf for         30
me. But my younger brother left the house and
squandered all his property with drunkards, and
you have now killed the calf for him.' And the
father said: 'You are always with me, and all         31
mine is yours; and you should not be offended,         32
but should be glad that your brother was dead
and has become alive, was lost and is found.'

"A master planted a garden, cultivated it,         Mk. xii. 1
arranged it, did everything so that the garden
might yield as much fruit as possible. And he
sent laborers into the garden, that they might
work there, and gather the fruit, and pay him
according to the agreement for the garden. (The

master is the Father; the garden, the world; the laborers, men. The Father does no more than send His Son, the Son of Man, into the world, that men may yield fruit to the Father from the understanding of life which He placed in them.) The time came when the master sent a servant for the rents. (The Father, without ceasing, tells men that they must fulfill His will.) The laborers drove away the messenger of the master with nothing, and continued to live, imagining that the garden was their own, and that they themselves, of their own will, were settled on it. (Men drive away from themselves the declaration of the will of the Father, and continue to live, each one for himself, imagining that they live for the joys of the fleshly life.) Then the master sent one after another his chosen ones then his son, to remind the laborers of their debt. But the laborers quite lost their reason and imagined that if they killed this son of the master, who reminded them that the garden was not theirs, they would be left quite in peace. So they killed him.

"Thus men do not love even a reminder of the spirit which lives in them, and declares to

Mk. xii. 2

3

4-6

7

8

them that it is eternal and they are not eternal; and they have killed, as far as they could, the consciousness of the spirit; they have wrapped in a cloth and buried in the ground the talent that was given them.

"What, then, is the master to do? Nothing Mt. xxi. 40, 41 else than drive forth those laborers, and send others.

"What is the Father to do? Sow until there shall be fruit. And this He does.

"People have not understood and do not 42 understand that the consciousness of the spirit which is in them, and which they hide because it troubles them, brings life to them through understanding it. They reject that stone upon which 43 everything rests. And they who do not take as foundation the life of the spirit, do not enter into the kingdom of heaven, and do not receive life. In order to have faith, and to receive life, it is necessary to understand one's position, and not to expect rewards."

Then the disciples said to Jesus: "Increase Lk. xvii. 5 in us our faith. Tell us that which will make us more strongly believe in the life of the spirit, that we may not regret the life of the flesh, which must be given up wholly for the life of the spirit. For reward, you yourself say there is none."

Lk. xvii. 6    And in answer to this, Jesus said to them: "If you had such a faith as the faith that from a birch seed there springs up a great tree; if, also, you believed that in you there is the germ, the only germ, of the spirit whence springs up the true life, you would not ask me to increase in you your faith.

"Faith does not consist in believing something wonderful, but faith consists in understanding one's position, and wherein lies salvation. If you understand your position, you will not expect rewards, but will believe in that which is intrusted to you.

7    "When the master returns with the laborers from the field, he does not seat the laborer at
8   his table. But he bids him see to the cattle, and prepare his supper, and after this only says to
9   the laborer: 'Sit down, drink and eat.' The master will not thank the laborer for having done what he ought to do. And the laborer, if he understands that he is a laborer, is not offended,

but works, believing that he will receive his due.

"And so you, also, must fulfill the will of the Father, and think that we are worthless laborers, having only done what we ought to do, and not expect a reward, but be content with receiving that which is due to you. Lk. xvii. 10

"There is no need to take care to believe that there will be a reward, and life; this cannot be otherwise; but there is need to take care not to destroy this life, not to forget that it is given us that we may bring forth its fruits, and fulfill the will of the Father.

"And therefore always be ready, like servants awaiting a master, to answer him immediately when he comes. The servants do not know when he will return, either early or late, and they must always be ready. And when they meet the master, they have fulfilled his will, and it is well for them. xii. 35, 36 37, 38

"So in life also. Always, every minute of the present, you must live the life of the spirit, not thinking of the past or the future, and not saying to yourself: then or there I will do this or that.

Lk. xii. 39    "If the master knew when the thief would come, he would not sleep; and so do you also never sleep; because, to the life of the Son of Man time is nothing; he lives only in the present, and does not know when is the beginning or end of life.

t. xxiv. 45. 46    "Our life is the same as that of a slave whom the master has left as chief in his household. And well it is for that slave if he does the will of the master always! But if he shall say, 'The master will not soon return,' and shall forget the master's business, then the master will return unexpectedly, and will drive him out.

48

50

51

Mk. xiii. 33    "And so, be not downcast, but always live in the present by the spirit. For the life of the spirit there is no time.

Lk. xxi. 34    "Look to yourselves, so as not to weigh yourselves down, and not to blind yourselves with drunkenness, gluttony, and cares; so as not to let the time of salvation pass. The time of salvation, like a web, is cast over all; it is there always. And therefore always live the life of the Son of Man.

Mt. xxv. 1    "The kingdom of heaven is like this. Ten

maidens went with lamps to meet the bride-
groom. Five were wise and five foolish. The fool-  Mt. xxv. 2. 3
ish ones took lamps but did not take oil; but the  4
wise took lamps and a store of oil. While they  5
waited for the bridegroom, they went to sleep.
When the bridegroom was approaching, the fool-  6
ish maidens saw that they had little oil, and went  7
to buy some; and while they were gone, the  10
bridegroom came. And the wise maidens who
had oil went in with him, and the doors were
shut. Their business was only this, to meet the
bridegroom with lights; and the five foolish ones
forgot that it was important, not only that the
lights should burn, but that they should burn in
time. And in order that they might be burning
when the bridegroom came, they must burn without stopping.

"Life is only for this, to exalt the Son of
Man, and the Son of Man exists always. He is not
in time; and therefore, in serving him, one must
live without time, in the present alone.

"Therefore make efforts in the present to  Lk. xiii. 24
enter into the life of the spirit. If you do not  25
make these efforts you shall not enter. You will

say: 'We said so and so.' But there will be no good works to shows and there will not be life.

Mt. xvi. 27 Because the Son of Man, the one true spirit of life, will appear in each man, as such man has acted for the Son of Man.

Mt. xxv. 32 "Mankind is divided according to the way in which men serve the Son of Man. And by their works men shall be divided into two classes, as sheep are divided from goats in the flock. The one shall live, the other perish.

34 "They who have served the Son of Man, they shall receive that which belonged to them from the beginning of the world, that life which they have kept. They have kept life by the fact that they have served the Son of Man. They have fed the hungry, clothed the naked, welcomed the stranger, visited the prisoner. They have lived in the Son of Man, felt that he only is in all men, and therefore they have loved their neighbors.

"Whereas they who have not lived in the Son of Man, they have not served him, have not understood that he alone is in all, and therefore have not joined in him and have lost life in him, and have perished."

# 9

# Forgive Us Our Debts As We Forgive Our Debtors
## Temptations Conceal The True Life

*The illusions of temporal life conceal from men the true life in the present.*

ONCE, CHILDREN were brought to Jesus. His Mt. xix. 13 disciples began to drive the children away. Jesus saw this being done, and was grieved, and 14) said:—

"You drive the children away without reason. They are better than any, because children all live after the Father's will. They are, indeed, already in the kingdom of heaven. You should not drive them away, but learn from them; Lk. xviii. 17 because, in order to live in the Father's will, you must live as children live. Children do not abuse one another, do not bear ill-will to people, do not commit adultery, do not swear by anything, do not resist evil, do not go to law with any one, acknowledge no difference between their own people and foreigners. Therefore are they better than grown people, and are in the kingdom of heaven. If you do not refrain from all the temptations of the flesh, and become as children, you will not be in the kingdom of heaven.

"Only he who understands that children are better than we, because they do not break the Father's will, only he understands my teaching. And he who understands my teaching, he alone understands the Father's will. We cannot despise children, because they are better than we, and their hearts are pure in the sight of the Father, and are always with Him.

"And not one child perishes by the Father's will. They perish only as men entice them from the truth. And therefore it behooves us to take care of them, and not to entice them from the Father, and from true life.

"That man does ill who entices them from purity. To entice a child from good, to lead it into temptation, is as bad as to hang a millstone on its neck and throw it into the water. It is hard for it to swim to the surface; it is more likely to drown. It is as hard for a child to get out of temp-

*Mt. xviii. 3*

*5*

*Lk. ix. 48*

*Mt. xviii. 10*

*14*

tation into which a grownup man leads it.

"The world of men is unhappy only on Mt. xviii. 7 account of temptations. Temptations are everywhere in the world, they always were and always will be; and man perishes from temptations.

"Therefore give up everything, sacrifice 8 everything, if only you may not fall into temptation. A fox, if it fall into a trap, will wrench off its paw and go away, and the paw will heal and it will remain alive. Do you likewise. Give up everything, if only not to sink into temptation.

"Beware of temptation under that first Lk. xvii. 3 commandment; do not bear ill-will against men, when people offend you, and you would wish to be avenged on them.

"If a man offends you, remember that he is Mt. xviii. 15 the son of the same Father, and your brother. If he has offended you, go and persuade him of it face to face. If he listens to you, then you have the advantage, you will have found a new brother. If he does not listen to you, then call to your 16 aid two or three others who may persuade him. Lk. xvii. 4 And if he repents, forgive him. And if he offends you seven times, and seven times says, 'Forgive me,' then forgive him. But if he does not listen, then tell the society of believers in my teaching, and if he listens not to them, then forgive him, and have nothing to do with him.

"Because the kingdom of God is like this. A king began to settle with his tenants. And there was a man brought to him who owed him a million, and had nothing to pay him with. Then the king commanded to sell the man's estate, his wife, his children, and the man himself. But the tenant began to beg mercy of the king. And the king was gracious to him, and pardoned all his debt. And now this same tenant went home, and saw a peasant. This peasant owed him fifty shillings The king's tenant seized him, began to strangle him, and said: 'Give me what you owe me.' And the peasant fell at his feet, and said: 'Have patience with me, I will pay you all.' But the tenant showed him no mercy, and put the peasant into prison, to stay there until he paid everything. Other peasants saw this and went to the king, and told what the tenant had done. Then the king called the tenant, and said to him: 'Wicked creature, I pardoned you all your debt, because you prayed me. And you, also, should Mt. xviii. 33 have shown mercy to your debtor, because I showed mercy to you.' And the king became 34 angry, and gave the tenant to be made to suffer, until he should pay all his rent.

"Just so, the Father will do with you, if you 35 do not forgive, from the bottom of your heart, all those who are to blame in your sight.

"You know that if a quarrel arise with a v.25 man, it is better to make it up with him without going to the court. You know this, and you act so because you know, should it go to the court, you will lose more. Now, it is the same with all malice. If you know that malice is a bad thing, and removes you from the Father, then get clear of malice as soon as possible, and make your peace.

"You yourselves know that as you become Mt. xviii. 18 bound on earth, so you will be before the Father. And as you free yourselves on earth, so you will be also free before the Father. Understand that if 19 two or three on earth are united in my teaching, everything they may desire they already have from my Father. Because where two or three are 20 joined in the name of the spirit in man, the spirit of man is living in them.

Mk. x. 2      "Beware also of temptation under the second commandment; the temptation for men to change their wives."

Mt. xix. 3      There once came to Jesus orthodox teachers, who, trying him, said: "May a man leave his wife?"

4      He said to them: "From the very beginning man was created male and female. This was the

5   will of the Father. And therefore a man leaves father and mother and cleaves to his wife. And husband and wife unite in one body. So that the

6   wife is the same for a man as his own flesh. Therefore man must not break the natural law of God, and separate that which is united. According to your law of Moses, it is said that you may abandon a wife and take another; but this is untrue. According to the Father's will, this

9   is not so, and I tell you that he who casts off his wife drives into immorality both her, and him who shall have to do with her. And casting off his wife, a man breeds immorality in the world."

20      And the disciples said to Jesus: "It is too

hard to be tied for life, whatever happens, to one wife. If that must be, it were better not to marry."

He said to them: "You may refrain from marriage, but you must understand what you are about. If any one wishes to live without wife, let him be quite pure, and not approach women; but he who loves women, let him unite with one wife and not cast her off, and not gaze upon others. Mt. xix. 11 10

"Beware of temptation against the third commandment; the temptation to force people to fulfill obligations and to take oaths."

Once, tax-gatherers came to Peter, and asked him: "How about your teacher, does he pay taxes?" Peter said: "No, he does not." And he went and told Jesus that he had been stopped, and told that all were bound to pay taxes. xvii. 24 25

Then Jesus said to him: "The king does not take taxes of his sons; and moreover, men are not bound to pay any one but the king. Is this not so? Well, so it is with us. If we are sons of God, then we are bound to no one but God, and free from all obligations. And if they demand taxes of you, then pay. But do so, not because it 27 is your duty, but because you may not resist evil. Otherwise resistance to evil will cause a greater evil."

Mt. xxii. 16    Another time, the orthodox joined with Caesar's officials, and went to Jesus, to entrap him in his words. They said to him: "You teach every one according to the truth. Tell us, are we bound to pay taxes to Caesar or not?" Jesus understood that they wished to convict him of not acknowledging duty to Caesar. And he said to them: "Show me that with which you pay taxes to Caesar." They handed him a coin. He looked at the coin, and said: "What is this here? Whose effigy and whose signature are these?" They said: "Caesar's." And he said: "Well then, pay Caesar that which is Caesar's, but that which is God's, your soul, give to no one but to God." Money, goods, your labor, give everything to him who shall ask it of you. But your soul, give to none but God.

    "Your orthodox teachers go about everywhere, and compel people to swear and vow that they will fulfill the law. But by this they only pervert people, and make them worse than before.

It is impossible to promise with one's body for one's soul. In your soul, God is; therefore people cannot promise for God to men. <sup>Mt. xxiii. 16-20</sup>

"Beware. Temptation under the fourth commandment is the temptation for men to judge and execute people, and call upon others to take part in these judgments and executions."

The disciples of Jesus once went into a village, and asked for a night's lodging; but they were not admitted. Then the disciples went to Jesus to complain, and said: "Let these people be struck with lightning." Jesus said: "You still do not understand of what spirit you are. I am teaching, not how to destroy, but how to save people." <sup>Lk. ix. 52 / 53 / 54 / 55 / 56</sup>

Once a man came to Jesus, and said: "Bid my brother give me my inheritance." Jesus said to him: "No one has made me judge over you, and I judge no one. And neither may you judge any one." <sup>xii. 13 / 14</sup>

The orthodox once brought a woman to Jesus, and said: "See, this woman was taken in adultery. Now, by the law she should be stoned to death. What do you say?" <sup>Jn. viii. 3 / 4 / 5</sup>

Jn. viii. 6 Jesus answered nothing, and waited for
7 them to bethink themselves. But they pressed
him, and asked what he would adjudge to this
woman. Then he said: "He among you who is
8 without fault, let him be the first to cast a stone
at her." He said nothing more.

9 Then the orthodox looked within themselves, and their consciences smote them; and
they who were in front sought to get behind the
10 others, and all went away. And Jesus remained
alone with the woman. He looked round, and
saw that there was none else. "Well," said he to
the woman, "has no one condemned you?" She
11 said: "No one." Then he said: "And I do not condemn you. Go, and henceforth sin no more."

Beware. Temptation against the fifth commandment is the temptation for men to consider
themselves bound to do good only to their countrymen, and to consider foreigners as enemies.

Lk. x. 15 A teacher of the law wished to try Jesus,
and said: "What am I to do in order to receive
27 the true life?" Jesus said: "You know,—love your
Father, God, and him who is your brother
through your Father, God; of whatever country

he may be." And the teacher of the law said: Lk. x. 29 "This would be well, if there were not different nations; but as it is, how am I to love the enemies of my own people?"

And Jesus said: 'There was a Jew who fell 30 into misfortune. He was beaten, robbed, and abandoned on the road. A Jewish priest went by, 31 glanced at the wounded man, and went on. A Jewish Levite passed, looked at the wounded 32 man, and also went by. But there came a man of 33 a foreign, hostile nation, a Samaritan. This Samaritan saw the Jew, and did not think of the fact that Jews have no esteem for the Samaritans, but pitied the poor Jew. He washed 34 and bound his wounds, and carried him on his ass to an inn, paid money for him to the innkeep- 35 er, and promised to come again to pay for him. Thus shall you also behave toward foreign nations, toward those who hold you of no account and ruin you. Then you will receive true life."

Jesus said: "The world loves its own, and Mt. xvi. 21 hates God's people. Therefore men of the world—priests, preachers, officials will harass those who shall fulfill the will of the Father. And I am going to Jerusalem, and shall be persecuted and killed. But my spirit cannot be killed, but will remain alive."

Mk. viii. 32

Having heard that Jesus would be tortured and killed in Jerusalem, Peter was sad, and took Jesus by the hand, and said to him: "If so, then you had better not go to Jerusalem." Then Jesus said to Peter: "Do not say this. What you say is temptation. If you fear tortures and death for me, this means that you are not thinking of that which is godly, of the spirit, but are thinking of what is worldly."

34

And having called the people and his disciples, Jesus said: "He who wishes to live according to my teaching, let him forsake his fleshly life, and let him be ready for all fleshly suffering; because he who fears for his fleshly life, shall destroy the true life; he who despises the fleshly life, shall save the true life."

Mt. xxii. 23

And they did not understand this, and certain materialists coming, he explained to all what is the meaning of the true life and the awakening from death.

The materialists said that after the fleshly death there is no longer any life. They asked: <sub></sub> Mt. xxii. 24 "How can all rise from the dead? If all were to rise, then in rising they could in no way have life 25 together. For instance, there were seven brothers among us. The first married and died. The wife 28 was taken by the second brother and he died, and she was taken by the third, who also died, and so on unto the seventh. Well now, how shall these seven brothers live with one wife if all arise from the dead?"

Jesus said to them: "You either purposely Lk. xx. 34 confuse things, or you do not understand what the awakening to life is. Men in this present life marry. But they who shall earn everlasting life, 35 and the awakening from death, do not marry. And that because they can no longer die, but are 36 united with the Father. In your writings, it is said Mt. xxii. 31 that God said: 'I am the God of Abraham, Isaac, 32 and Jacob.' And this was said when Abraham, Isaac, and Jacob had died from among men. It follows, that they who have died from among men are alive to God. If God is, and God does not die, then they who are with God are always alive. The awakening from death is, to live in the will of the Father. For the Father, there is no time, therefore in fulfilling the will of the Father, in joining Him, man departs from time and death."

Mt. xxii. 34 When they heard this, the orthodox no longer knew what to devise to compel Jesus to hold his tongue; and together they began to question Jesus. And one of the orthodox said: "Teacher, what, in your opinion, is the chief commandment in the whole law?"

The orthodox thought that Jesus would get confused in the answer about the law. But Jesus said: "It is, to love the Lord with all one's soul, in whose power we are. From it the second commandment follows, which is, to love one's neighbor. Because the same Lord is in him. And this is the substance of all that is written in all your books."

And Jesus said further: "In your opinion, what is Christ? Is he some one's son?" They said: "In our opinion, Christ is the son of David." Then he said to them: "How, then does David call Christ his Lord? Christ is neither son of

David, nor any one's son after the flesh; but Christ is that same Lord, our Ruler, whom we know in ourselves as our life. Christ is that understanding which is in us."

And Jesus said: "See, beware of the leaven of orthodox teachers. And beware of the leaven of the materialists and of the leaven of the government. But most of all, beware of the leaven of the self-styled 'orthodox,' because in them is the chief stumbling-block."

And when the people understood of what he was speaking, he repeated: "Most of all, beware of the teaching of the scholars, of the self-called 'orthodox.' Beware of them, because they have taken the place of the prophets who declared the will of God to the people. They have perversely assumed authority to preach to the people the will of God. They preach words, and do nothing. And the result is that they do no more than say: 'Do this and that.' And there is no further result, because they do nothing good, but only talk. And they tell people to do what is impossible to be done, and they themselves do nothing. They only labor to keep the teaching in their own hands; and with this aim they strive to appear imposing; they dress themselves up and exalt themselves. Know, therefore, that no one should call himself teacher and leader. But the self-styled orthodox are called teachers, and by this very thing they hinder you from entering into the kingdom of heaven, where they themselves do not enter. These orthodox think that people may be brought to God by exterior rites and pledges. Like blind men, they do not see that the outside show means nothing; that all depends upon the soul of man. They do the easiest thing, the external thing; that which is needful and diffi- cult—love, compassion, truth—they leave undone. It suffices them to be only outwardly in the law, and to bring others outwardly to the law. And therefore they, like painted coffins, outward- ly look clean, but are an abomination within. They outwardly honor the holy martyrs. But in every deed they are the same as those who tor- ture and kill the saints. They were before, and are now, the enemies of all good. From them comes all the evil in the world; because they hide the good, and instead of it uphold evil. Most of all to be feared, therefore, are self-called teachers. Because you yourselves know every mistake may be made good. But if people are mistaken as to what good is, this mistake can never be set right. And this is precisely the condition of self-called leaders."

And Jesus said: "I wished, here in Jerusalem, to join all men in one understanding of true happiness; but the people here are only capable of putting to death the teachers of good. And therefore they will remain the same godless people as they were, and will not know the true God; until they shall lovingly welcome the understanding of God." And Jesus went away from the temple.

Then his disciples said to him: "But what will happen to this temple of God, with all its embellishments which people have brought into it, to give to God." And Jesus said: "I tell you truly, the whole of this temple, with all its embellishments, shall be destroyed, and nothing shall remain of it. There is one temple of God; that is, the hearts of men when they love each other."

And they asked him: "When shall there be

Mk. III. 29

Mt. xxiii. 37

38

39

xxiv. 1

2

Forgive Us Our Debts As We Forgive Our Debtors

such a temple?" And Jesus said to them: "That
4 will not be soon. People will yet long be
deceived in the name of my teaching, and wars
and rebellions will be the result. And there will
10 be great lawlessness, and little love. But when
the true teaching shall spread among all men,
14 then will be the end of evil and temptations."

# 10

## Lead Us Not Into Temptation
### The Warfare With Temptation

*Therefore, not to fall by temptation, we must, at every
moment of life, be at one with the Father*

AFTER THIS, THE ORTHODOX chief priests Lk. xi. 53
began to do all they could to lay traps for Jesus,
in some way or other to destroy him. They gath- Jn. xi. 47
ered in council, and began to consider. They 48
said: "This man must somehow or other be put
an end to. He so proves his teaching that, if he
be left alone, all will believe in him, and cast off
our belief. Already half of the people believe in
him. But if the Jews believe in his teaching, that
all men are sons of one Father, and brothers,
and that there is nothing in our Hebrew people
different from other peoples, then the Romans
will completely overwhelm us, and the Hebrew
kingdom will be no more."

And the orthodox high priests and learned Lk. xix. 47

men for long counseled together, and could not

Lk. xix. 48 think what to do with Jesus. They could not make up their minds to kill him.

Jn. xl. 49 Then one of them, Caiaphas, the chief priest of that year, thought of the following

50 device. He said to the others: "You must remember this: it is expedient to kill one man, that the whole people may not perish. If we leave this man alone, the people will perish; this I declare

52 to you. Therefore it is better to kill Jesus. Even if the people do not perish, they will nevertheless go astray, departing from the one belief, if we do not kill Jesus. Therefore it is better to kill Jesus."

53 And when Caiaphas said this, they resolved that there was no need to discuss, but that Jesus must be killed without fail.

54 They would have taken Jesus at once and killed him, but he withdrew from them into the

55 desert. But at this time the feast of the Passover was approaching, when a great multitude always

56 gathered in Jerusalem. And the orthodox high priests reckoned upon Jesus coming with the

57 people to the feast. And they made known to the people that if any one should see Jesus he

should bring him to them.

And it so happened that, six days before Jn. xii. 1
the Passover, Jesus said to his disciples: "Let us xi. 7
go to Jerusalem." And he went with them.

And the disciples said to him: "Do not go 8
into Jerusalem. The high priests have resolved
now to stone you to death. If you come they will
kill you."

Jesus said to them: "I can fear nothing, 9
because I live in the light of understanding. And
as every man, that he may not stumble, walks by
day and not by night, so every man that he may
doubt nothing and fear nothing, must live by this
understanding. Only he doubts and fears who 10
lives by the flesh; but he who lives by understanding, for him there is nothing doubtful or
fearful."

And Jesus came to the village of Bethany, xii. 1
near Jerusalem, and to the house of Martha and
Mary which was there.

Early in the morning Jesus went into 10
Jerusalem. There was a great crowd for the feast.
And when they recognized Jesus, they surround- 13
ed him, tore branches from the trees and threw

their clothes before him on the road, and all shouted: "Here is our true king, he who has taught us the true God."

Jn. xii. 14    Jesus sat upon an ass's foal, riding, and the people ran before him and shouted; thus he

Mt. xxi. 10    rode into Jerusalem. And when he had thus ridden into the town, the whole people were excit-

11    ed, and asked: "Who is he?" They who knew him answered: "Jesus, the prophet of Nazareth, in Galilee."

Mk. xi. 15    And Jesus went into the temple, and again drove out thence all the buyers and sellers.

Jn. xii. 19    And the orthodox high priests saw all this, and said to each other: "See what this man is doing. The whole people are following him."

Mk. xi. 18    But they did not dare to take him straight from among the people, because they saw that the people were gathering round him, and they bethought them how to take him by cunning.

Jn. xii. 20    Meanwhile Jesus was in the temple, and taught the people. Among the people, besides Jews, there were Greeks and heathen. The Greeks heard of the teaching of Jesus, and understood his teaching in this way, namely, that he taught the truth, not only to Hebrews but to all men. Therefore they wished to be also his disciples, and spoke about this to Philip. And Philip told this to Andrew. Jn. xii. 21

22

These two disciples feared to bring Jesus together with the Greeks. They were afraid lest the people should be angry with Jesus, because he did not recognize any difference between Hebrews and other nations, and they long wavered about telling this to Jesus; but afterward both together told him, and hearing that the Greeks wished to be his followers, Jesus was troubled. He knew that the people hated him because he made no difference between the Hebrews and the heathen, but acknowledged himself to be the same as the heathen.

He said: "The hour is come to explain what I understand by the Son of Man, though I perish because, in explaining this, I destroy distinction between Jews and heathen. I must speak the truth. A grain of wheat will only bring forth fruit when it itself perishes. He who loves his fleshly life loses the true life, and he who despises the fleshly life keeps it for the everlasting life. He 23 24 25

Jn. xii. 26  who wishes to follow my teaching, let him do as I do. And he who does as I do shall be rewarded

27  by my Father. My soul is now wrestling. Shall I surrender myself to the compromises of temporary life or fulfill the will of the Father, now, at this hour? And what then? Surely now, when this hour is come in which I am living, I shall not say: 'Father, save me from that which I should do.' I cannot say this for the sake of my life. And there-

28  fore I say: 'Father, show yourself in me.'"

31  And Jesus said: "Henceforth the present society of men is condemned to destruction. From now that which rules this world shall be

32  destroyed. And when the Son of Man shall be exalted above the earthly life, then shall he unite all in one."

34  Then the Jews said to him: "We understand from the law what the everlasting Christ is; but why do you say that the Son of Man shall be exalted? What is the meaning of exalting the Son of Man?"

35  To this Jesus answered: "To exalt the Son of Man, means to live by the life of understand-

36  ing that is in you. To exalt the Son of Man above

that which is earthly, means to believe in the light while there is light, in order to be a son of understanding.

"He who believes in my teaching believes <sub></sub> Jn. xii. 44 not in me, but in that spirit which gave life to the world. And he who understands my teaching, 45 understands that spirit which gave life to the world. But if any one hears my words and does 47 not fulfill them, it is not I who blame him, seeing that I came, not to accuse, but to save. He who 48 does not accept my words is accused, not by my teaching, but by the understanding which is in himself. This it is which accuses him. I did not 49 speak of myself, but said what my Father, the living spirit in me, suggested to me. That which I 50 say, the spirit of understanding has told me, and that which I teach is the true life."

And having said this, Jesus went away, and 36 again hid from the chief priests.

And of those who heard these words of 42 Jesus, many of the powerful and wealthy people believed, but were afraid to acknowledge it to the chief priests, because not one of these priests believed and acknowledged it. They were accustomed to judge according to man, and not according to God.

After Jesus had hidden, the high priests and the elders again met in the court of

4 Caiaphas. And they began to plan how to take

5 Jesus unknown to the people, for they were

14 afraid to seize him openly. And there came to their council one of the first twelve disciples of

15 Jesus, Judas Iscariot, who said: "If you wish to take Jesus secretly, so that the people may not see, I will find a time when there will be few people with him, and will show you where he is; and then take him. But what will you give me for

16 this?" They promised him for this thirty silver coins. He agreed; and from that time began to seek an opportunity to bring the chief priests upon Jesus, in order to take him.

17 Meanwhile Jesus withdrew from the people, and with him were only his disciples. When the first feast of unleavened bread approached, the disciples said to Jesus: "Where, then, shall

18 we keep the Passover?" And Jesus said: "Go into some village, and enter some one's house, and say that we have not time to prepare the feast,

and ask him to admit us to celebrate the Passover." And the disciples did so; they asked a <sub>Mt. xxvi. 19</sub> man in the village, and he invited them in. And they came and sat down to the table, Jesus and <sub>20</sub> the twelve disciples, Judas among them.

Jesus knew that Judas Iscariot had already <sub>Jn. xiii. 11</sub> promised to betray him to death, but he did not accuse Judas for this, or show him ill-will but as in all his life he taught his disciples love, so even now he only reproached Judas lovingly. When they all twelve were seated at table, he looked at <sub>Mt. xxvi. 21</sub> them, and said: "Among you sits he who has <sub>Mk. xiv. 18</sub> betrayed me. Yes, he who eats and drinks with <sub>Mt. xxvi. 23</sub> me shall also destroy me." And he said nothing more, so that they did not know of whom he spoke, and they began to sup.

When they began to eat, Jesus took a loaf <sub>26</sub> and broke it into twelve parts, and gave each of the disciples a piece, and said: "Take and eat, this is my body." And he then filled a cup with <sub>27</sub> wine, handed it to the disciples, and said: "Drink, all of you, of this cup." And when they had all drunk, he said: "This is my blood. I shed it that <sub>28</sub> people may know my will, to forgive others their <sub>Lk. xxii. 18</sub>

sins. For I shall soon die, and be no more with you in this world, but shall join you only in the kingdom of heaven."

After this, Jesus got up from the table, girt himself with a towel, took a ewer of water and began to wash the feet of all the disciples. And he came to Peter; and Peter said: "But why will you wash my feet?" Jesus said to him: "It seems strange to you that I should wash your feet; but you will know soon why I do this. Though you are clean, yet not all of you are so, but among you is my betrayer, to whom I gave, with my own hand, bread and wine, and whose feet I wish to wash."

When Jesus had washed all their feet, he again sat down, and said: "Do you understand why I did this? It was so that you always may do the same for each other. I, your teacher, do this, that you may know how to behave toward those who do you evil. If you have understood this, and will do it, then you will be happy. When I said that one of you will betray me, I did not speak of all of you, because only a single one of you, whose feet I washed, and who ate bread with me, will betray me."

And having said this, Jesus was troubled in spirit, and yet again said: "Yes, yes, one of you will betray me." <sub>Jn. xii. 21</sub>

And again the disciples began to look round at each other, not knowing of whom he spoke. One disciple sat near to Jesus, and Simon Peter signed to him in a way to ask who the betrayer was. The disciple asked. And Jesus said: "I will soak a piece of bread, and give it to him: and he to whom I shall give it is my betrayer." And he gave the bread to Judas Iscariot, and said to him: "What you wish to do, do quickly." Then Judas understood that he must go out, and as soon as he had taken the bread he forthwith went out. And it was impossible to follow him, as it was night.

And when Judas was gone out, Jesus said: "It is now clear to you what the Son of Man is. It is now clear to you that in him God is, to make him as blessed as God Himself.

"Children! I have not long now to be with you. Do not equivocate over my teaching, as I said to the orthodox, but do that which I do. I

Jn. xlll. 34 give you this, a new commandment. As I always, and to the end, have loved you all, do you always, and to the end, love each other. By this only will you be distinguished. Seek to be only thus distinguished from other people. Love one another."

Mt. xxvi. 30 And after this, they went to the Mount of Olives.

31 And on the way Jesus said to them: "See, the time is coming when that shall happen which is written, the shepherd shall be killed, and all the sheep shall be scattered. And tonight this shall happen. I shall be taken and you will all abandon me, and scatter."

33 Peter said to him in answer: "Even if all shall be frightened, and scatter, I will not deny you. I am ready for prison and for death with you."

34 And Jesus said to him: "But I tell you that this very night, before cockcrow, after I have been taken, you will deny me, not once, but thrice."

35 But Peter said that he would not deny him; and the other disciples averred the same.

Then Jesus said to the disciples: "Before, <small>Lk. xxii. 35</small> neither I nor you had need of anything. You went without wallet and without change of shoes, and I so bade you do. But now, if I am accounted an <small>36</small> outlaw, we can no longer do so, but we must be furnished with everything, and with swords, that we may not perish in vain."

And the disciples said: "See, we have two swords." <small>38</small>

Jesus said: "It is well."

And having said this, Jesus went with the followers into the garden of Gethsemane. <small>Mt. xxvi. 36</small> Coming into the garden, he said: "Wait you here, <small>Jn. xviii. 1</small> but I wish to pray."

And while near to Peter and the two brothers, sons of Zebedee, he began to feel weary and <small>Mt. xxvi. 37</small> sad, and he said to them: "I feel very sad and my soul is full of the anguish before death. Wait <small>38</small> here, and be not cast down as I am."

And he went off a little way, lay on the ground on his face, and began to pray, and said: <small>39</small> "My Father, the Spirit! Let it be not as I will, which is that I should not die, but let it be as Thou wilt. Let me die, but for Thee, as a spirit, all is possible; let it be that I may not fear death, that I may escape the temptation of the flesh."

And then he arose, went up to the disci-

Mt. xxvi. 40 ples, and saw that they were cast down. And he said to them: "How is it you have not strength for one hour to keep up your spirit even as I! Keep

41 up your spirit, so as not to fall into the temptation of the flesh. The spirit is strong, the flesh is weak."

And again Jesus went away from them,

42 and again began to pray, and said: "Father, if I must suffer, must die, and am about to die, then so let it be. Let Thy will be done." And having

43 said this, he again went up to the disciples, and saw that they were still more cast down, and ready to weep.

And he again went away from them, and

44 the third time said: "Father, let Thy will be done."

Then he returned to the disciples, and said

45 to them: "Now be easy, and be calm, because it is now decided that I shall give myself into the hands of worldly men."

---

# 11

## Deliver Us From Evil
### The Farewell Discourse

*The self-life is an illusion which comes through the flesh,*
*an evil. The true life is the life common to all men.*

AND PETER SAID to Jesus: "Whither are you Jn. xiii. 36
going?"

Jesus answered: "You will not have the
strength now to go whither I am going; but afterward you will go the same way."

And Peter said: "Why do you think that I 37
have not the strength now to follow whither you
go? I will give up my life for you."

And Jesus said: "You say that you will give 38
up your life for me, and yet even before cockcrow you shall deny me thrice." And Jesus said xiv. 1
to the disciples: "Be not troubled and be not
afraid, but believe in the true God of life and in
my teaching.

---
190

Jn. xiv. 2 "The life of the Father is not only that
which is on earth, but there is another life also. If
there were only such a life as the life here, I
would say to you, that when I die I shall go into
Abraham's bosom, and make ready a place there
for you, and I shall come and take you, and we
shall together live happily in Abraham's bosom.
But I point out to you only the direction to life."

Thomas said: "But we do not know whither
you go, and therefore we cannot know the way.
We want to know what there will be after death."

Jesus said: "I cannot show you what will
be there; my teaching is the way, and the truth
and the life. And it is impossible to be joined
with the Father of life otherwise than through my
teaching. If you fulfill my teaching, you shall
know the Father."

Philip said: "But who is the Father?"

And Jesus said: "The Father is He who
gives life. I have fulfilled the will of the Father,
and therefore by my life you may know wherein
is the will of the Father. I live by the Father, and
the Father lives in me. All that I say and do, I do
by the will of the Father. My teaching is, that I am

in the Father and the Father is in me. If you do not understand my teaching, yet you see me and my works. And therefore you may understand what the Father is. And you know that he who *Jn. xiv. 12* shall follow my teaching may do the same as I; and yet more, because I shall die, but he will still *13* live. He who shall live according to my teaching, shall have all that he wishes, because then the Son will be one with the Father. Whatever you *14* may wish that accords with my teaching, all that you shall have. But for this you must love my *15* teaching. My teaching will give you, in my place, *16* an intercessor and comforter. This comforter will *17* be the consciousness of truth, which worldly men do not understand; but you will know it in yourselves. You never will be alone, if the spirit *18* of my teaching is with you. I shall die, and world- *19* ly men will not see me; but you will see me because my teaching lives and you will live by it. And then, if my teaching shall be in you, you will *20* understand that I am in the Father and the Father in me. He who shall fulfill my teaching, *21* shall feel in himself the Father; and in him my spirit shall live."

Jn. xiv. 22 And Judas, not Iscariot, but another, said to him: "But why, then, may not all live by the spirit of truth?"

23 Jesus said in answer: "Only he who fulfills my teaching, only him the Father loves, and in 24 him only can my spirit abide. He who does not fulfill my teaching, him my Father cannot love, because this teaching is not mine, but the 25 Father's. This is all that I can tell you now. But 26 my spirit, the spirit of truth, which shall take up its abode in you after I am gone, shall reveal to you all, and you shall recall and understand 27 much of that which I have told you. So that you may always be calm in spirit, not with that worldly calm which men of the world seek, but with 28 that calm of spirit in which we no longer fear anything. On this account, if you fulfill my teaching, you have no reason to grieve over my death. I, as the spirit of truth, will come to you, and, together with the knowledge of the Father, will take up my abode in your heart. If you fulfill my teaching, then you must rejoice, because instead of me you will have the Father with you in your heart, and this is better for you.

"My teaching is the tree of life. The Father <sub></sub> Jn. xv. 2
is He who tends the tree. He prunes and cherish- 3
es those branches upon which there is fruit, that
they may yield more. Keep my teaching of life, 4
and life will be in you. And as a shoot lives not of
itself, but out of the tree, so do you live by my
teaching. My teaching is the tree, you are the 5
shoots. He who lives by my teaching of life yields
much fruit; and without my teaching there is no
life. He who does not live by my teaching withers 6
and dies; and the dry branches are cut off and
burnt.

"If you will live by my teaching, and fulfill 7
it, then you shall have all that you desire. 8
Because the will of the Father is, that you may
live the true life and have that which you desire.
As the Father gave me happiness, so I give you 9
happiness. Hold to this happiness. I am living,
because the Father loves me and I love the 10
Father; do you also live by the same love. If you 11
will live by this, you shall be blessed.

"My commandment is, that you love one 12
another as I have loved you. There is no greater 13
love than to sacrifice one's life for the love of

'one's own, as I have done.

Jn. xv. 14 "You are my equals, if you do that which I

15 have taught you. I do not hold you as slaves, to whom orders are given, but as equals; because I have made clear to you all that I have known of

16 the Father. You do not, of your own will, choose my teaching; but because I have pointed out to you that only truth by which you will live, and from which you will have all that you wish.

17 "The teaching is summed up in this—Love one another.

18 "If the world should hate you, then do not

19 wonder; it hates my teaching. If you were at one with the world, it would love you. But I have sev-

20 ered you from the world, and for that it will hate

21 you. If they persecuted me, they will persecute you also. They will do all this, because they do

22 not know the true God. I explained to them, but

23 they did not wish to hear me. They did not understand my teaching, because they did not

24 understand the Father. They saw my life, and my

25 life showed them their error. And for this they

26 still more hated me. The spirit of truth which shall come to you will confirm this to you. And

you will accept it. I tell you this beforehand, so Jn. xvi. 27
that you may not be deceived when persecutions Jn. xvi. 1
shall be upon you. You shall be made outcasts; 2
men shall think that in killing you they do God's
pleasure. All this they cannot help doing, 3
because they understand neither my teaching
nor the true God. All this I tell you beforehand, 4
so that you may not wonder when it comes
about.

"Well then, I now go away to that Spirit 5
which sent me; and now you understand, you
need not ask me whither I go. But before, you 6
were grieved that I did not tell you whither, to
what place, I depart.

"But I tell you truly that it is well for you 7
that I am going. If I do not die, the spirit of truth
will not appear to you, but if I die, it will take up
its abode in you. It will take up its abode in you, 8
and it will be clear to you where untruth is,
where truth is, and how to make decision. 9
Untruth, in that people do not believe in the life
of the spirit. Truth, in that I am one with the 10
Father. Decision, in that the power of, the fleshly 11
life is at an end.

"I would say yet much more to you, but it
13   is difficult for you to understand. But when the
spirit of truth dwells in you, it will show you the
whole truth, because it will tell you, not a new
thing of its own, but that which is of God; and it
will show you the way in all concerns of life. It
15   also will be from the Father, as I am from the
Father therefore it also will tell you the same as I
tell you.

16      "But when I, the spirit of truth, shall be in
you, you will not always see me. Sometimes you
will, and sometimes you will not, hear me."

17      And the disciples said one to another:
"What does he mean when he says. 'Sometimes
you will see me, sometimes you will not see me.'
18   What means this, 'Sometimes you will, sometimes you will not?'"

19      Jesus said to them: "Do you not understand what this means, 'Sometimes you will,
sometimes you will not see me?' You know how
20   it always is in the world, that some are sad and
grieved, while others rejoice. And you will grieve,
21   but your grief will pass into Joy. A woman, when
she bears, grieves while she is in the pangs of

childbirth; but when that is ended, she does not remember the pangs, for joy that a man is born into the world. And so you will grieve; presently <sub>Jn. xvi. 22</sub> you will see me, the spirit of truth will enter into you, and your grief will be turned into joy. Then you will no longer ask anything of me, because 23 you will have all that you wish. Then all which one of you desires in the spirit, all that he will have from his Father.

"You formerly asked for nothing for the 24 spirit; but now ask what you will for the spirit, and you will have all; so that your bliss will be 25 full. Now I, as a man, cannot tell you this clearly in words, but when I, as the spirit of truth, shall live in you, I will proclaim to you clearly about the Father. Then it will not be I who will give you 26 all you ask of the Father in the name of the spirit. But the Father will Himself give, because He 27 loves you for having received my teaching. You have understood that understanding proceeds 28 from the Father into the world and returns from the world to the Father."

Then the disciples said to Jesus: "Now we 29 have understood everything, and have nothing

Jn. xvi. 30 more to ask, we believe that you are from God."

33 And Jesus said: "All that I have said to you is in order that you may have confidence and rest in my teaching. Whatever ills may befall you in the world, fear nothing: my teaching will conquer the world."

xvii. 1 After this, Jesus raised his eyes to heaven, and said:

"My Father! Thou hast given Thy Son the freedom of life in order that he may receive the 3 true life. Life is the knowledge of the true God of the understanding, Who is discovered to me. I 6 have discovered Thee to men on earth; I have 4 done that work which Thou hast bidden me do. I 6 have shown Thy being to men on earth. They were Thine before, but by Thy will I have discov- 7. 8 ered to them the truth, and they know Thee. They have understood that all they have, their life, is from Thee only, and that I have taught them, not of myself, but as proceeding, I with 9 them, from Thee. But I pray to Thee for those 10. 11 who acknowledge Thee. They have understood that all that I have is Thine, and all that is Thine is mine. I am no longer in the world, for I return to Thee; but they are in the world, and therefore I pray Thee, Father, to preserve in them Thy under- Jn. xvii. 15 standing. I do not pray Thee to remove them from the world but to free them from evil; to confirm them in Thy truth. Thy understanding is the 17, 18 truth My Father! I wish them to be as I am; to 22 understand as I do, that the true life began before the beginning of the world. That they should all be one; as Thou, Father, art in me, and I in Thee, so they may also be one in me. I in them, Thou in me, so that all may be one; so that 23 all men may understand they are not self-created, but that Thou, in love, hast sent them into the world as Thou didst send me Father of truth! The world did not know Thee; but I knew 25 Thee, and they have known Thee through me. And I have made plain to them what Thou art. 26 Thou art in me, that the love with which Thou hast loved me may be in them also. Thou gavest them life, and therefore didst love them. I have taught them to know this, and to love Thee; so that Thy love might be returned from them to Thee."

# 12

# Thine Is The Kingdom, The Power, And The Glory
## Union With The Spirit

*Therefore, for him who lives, not the self-life, but a com-
mon life in the will of the Father, there is no death. Bodily
death is for him union with the Father.*

Mt. xxvi. 46 AFTER THIS, JESUS SAID: "Now arise, and
let us go; already he is coming who will betray
me."

47　　And he had hardly said this,when suddenly
Judas, one of the twelve disciples, appeared, and
48　with him a great throng of people with sticks and
swords. Judas said to them: "I will bring you
where he and his followers are, and so that you
may know him among them all, he whom I shall
49　first kiss, that is he." And he straightway went up
to Jesus, and said: "Hail, teacher!" and kissed
him.

50　　And Jesus said to him: "Friend, why are
you here?"

---

Then the guard surrounded Jesus, and wished to take him.

And Peter snatched the sword from the Mt. xxvi. 51 high priest's servant, and slashed the man's ear.

But Jesus said: "You must not oppose evil. 52 Cease." And he said to Peter: "Return the sword to him from whom you took it; he who shall draw the sword, shall perish with the sword."

And after this, Jesus turned to the crowd, 55 and said: "Why have you come out against me, as against a robber, with arms? I was every day among you in the temple, and taught you, and you did not take me. But now is your hour, and Lk. xxii. 53 the power of darkness."

Then, having seen that he was taken, all Mt. xxvi. 56 the disciples ran away.

And the officer ordered the soldiers to Jn. xviii. 12 take Jesus, and bind him. The soldiers bound him, and took him first to Annas. This was the 13 father-in-law of Caiaphas, and Caiaphas was the high priest for that year, and lived in the same house with Annas. This was the same Caiaphas 14 who planned how to destroy Jesus. He held that it was good for the sake of the people to destroy

Mk. xiv. 53 Jesus, because, if that were not done, it would be worse for the whole people. And they took Jesus to the house where this high priest lived.

Mt. xxvi. 58 When they had brought Jesus thither, one of his disciples, Peter, followed him from afar, and watched where they were taking him. When they brought Jesus into the court of the high priest, Peter went in also, to see how all would

69 end. And a girl in the yard saw Peter, and said to him: "You, also, were with Jesus of Galilee."

70 Then Peter was afraid that they would accuse him also, and he said aloud before all the people: " I do not know what you are talking about."

71 Afterward, when they had taken Jesus into the house, Peter also entered the hall, with the people. In the hall, a woman was warming herself at the fire, and Peter approached. The woman looked at Peter, and said to the people: "See, this man is likely to have been with Jesus of

72 Nazareth." Peter was still more frightened, and swore that he never was with him, and did not

73 even know what kind of a man Jesus was. A little while after, the people came up to Peter, and said: "It is quite clear that you also were among

---

the disturbers. By your speech one may know that you are from Galilee." Then Peter began to Mt. xxvi. 74 swear, and aver that he had never known or seen Jesus.

And he had hardly said this, when the cock 75 crew. And Peter remembered those words which Jesus had said to him, when Peter swore that if all denied Jesus, he would not deny him: "Before the cock crow this night, you will deny me thrice." And Peter went out, and cried bitterly. Jesus had prayed that he might not thus fall into temptation. He had fallen into one temptation, that of strife, when he began to defend Jesus; and into another temptation, the fear of death, when he denied Jesus.

And there gathered to the high priest, the Mk. xiv. 53 orthodox chief priests, assistants, and officials. And when all were assembled, they brought in Jn. xviii. 19 Jesus; and the chief priests asked him, what was his teaching, and who were his followers.

And Jesus answered: "I always said all I 20 had to say before everybody openly, and so I speak now; I concealed nothing from any one, and I conceal nothing now. But about what do 21 you question me? Question those who heard and understood my teaching. They will tell you."

Jn. xviii. 22 When Jesus had said this, one of the high priest's servants struck him in the face, and said: "To whom are you speaking? Is this the way to answer the high priest?"

23 Jesus said: "If I spoke ill, say what I spoke ill. But if I said nothing ill, then there is no cause to beat me."

The orthodox chief priests strove to Mt. xxvi. 59 accuse Jesus, and at first did not find any proofs against him for which it was possible to condemn him. Afterward they found two witnesses. 60. 61 These said about Jesus: "We ourselves heard how this man said: 'I will destroy this temple of yours made with hands, and in three days will build up another temple to God, not made with 59 hands.'" But this evidence, also, was not enough 62 to condemn him. And therefore the high priest called up Jesus, and said: "Why do you not answer their evidence?"

63 Jesus held his tongue, saying nothing. Then the high priest said to him: "Well, say then, Are you the Christ, and of God?"

Jesus answered him, and said: "Yes, I am the Christ, and of God. You yourselves will now see that the Son of Man is made like God."

Then the high priest cried out: "You blaspheme! Now we do not want any evidence. We all hear, now, that you are a blasphemer." And the high priest turned to the assembly, and said: "You have yourselves heard that he blasphemes God. To what do you sentence him for this?"

And all said: "We sentence him to death."

Then all the people, and the guards, fell upon Jesus, and began to spit in his face, to strike him on the cheeks, and to tear at him. They covered his eyes, hit him in the face; and asked: "Now, prophet, guess who it was that hit you?"

But Jesus held his peace.

Having abused him, they took him, bound, to Pontius Pilate. And they brought him into the court.

Pilate, the governor, came out to them and asked: "Of what do you accuse this man?"

They said: "This man is doing wrong, so we have brought him to you."

Jn. xviii. 31     And Pilate said to them: "But if he does wrong, then judge him yourselves according to your law."

And they said: "We have brought him to you that you might execute him, for we are not allowed to kill any one."

32     And so that happened which Jesus expected. He said that one must be ready to die on the cross at the hands of the Romans, more likely than at the hands of the Jews.

Lk. xxiii. 2     And when Pilate asked, whereof they accused him, they said, that he was guilty of stirring up the people, and that he forbade the payment of taxes to Caesar, and that he set up himself as Christ and king.

Jn. xviii. 33     Pilate listened to them, and bade Jesus be brought to him in the court. When Jesus came in, Pilate said to him: "So you are king of the Jews?"

34     Jesus said to him: "Do you really suppose that I am a king, or are you repeating only that which others have told you?"

35     Pilate said: "I am not a Jew, therefore you cannot be my king, but your people have

---
207

brought you to me. What kind of a man are you?"

Jesus answered: "I am a king; but my king- Jn. xviii. 36 dom is not an earthly one. If I were an earthly king, my subjects would fight for me, and would not yield to the high priests. But as it is, you see that my kingdom is not an earthly one."

Pilate said to this: "But yet, do you not con- 37 sider yourself a king?" Jesus said: "Not only I, but you also, cannot but consider me a king. For I only teach, in order to discover to all the truth of the kingdom of heaven. And every one who lives by the truth, is a king."

Pilate said: "You spoke of truth. What is truth?" 38

And having said this, he turned, and went to the chief priests. He went out and said to them: "In my opinion, this man has done no wrong."

But the chief priests insisted upon their Mk. xv. 3 opinion, and said that he was doing much evil, and stirring up the people, and had raised the whole of Judea right from Galilee.

Then Pilate, in the presence of the chief 4

priests, began to question Jesus. But Jesus did not answer. Pilate then said to him: "Do you hear of what they accuse you? Why do you not justify yourself?"

Mk. xv. 5     But Jesus still held his tongue, and said not another word, so that Pilate wondered at him.

Lk. xxiii. 6     Pilate remembered that Galilee was in the power of King Herod, and asked: "Ah! he is from Galilee?" They answered: "Yes."

7     Then he said: "If he is from Galilee, then he is under the authority of Herod, and I will send him to him." Herod was then in Jerusalem, and Pilate, in order to rid himself, sent Jesus to Herod.

8     When they brought Jesus to Herod, Herod was very glad to see him. He had heard much of him, and wished to know what kind of man he Lk. xxiii. 9 was. So he called Jesus to him, and began to question him about all he wished to know. But 10 Jesus answered him nothing. And the chief priests and teachers, just as with Pilate, so before Herod, vehemently accused Jesus, and 11 said that he was a rioter. And Herod deemed

Jesus an empty fellow, and to mock him, bade them clothe him in red, and send him back to Pilate. Herod was pleased at Pilate's showing <sub>Lk. xxiii. 12</sub> respect to him, by sending Jesus for his judgment, and on this account they became friends, whereas formerly they had been at variance.

Now, when they brought Jesus again to <sub>13</sub> Pilate, Pilate called back the chief priests and Jewish authorities, and said to them: "You brought this man to me for stirring up the <sub>14</sub> people, and I have examined him before you, and do not see that he is a rioter. I sent him with you to Herod, and now, see,—nothing wrong is <sub>15</sub> found in him. And, in my opinion, there is no cause to punish him with death. Had you not better punish him and let him go?"

But when the chief priests heard this, all <sub>Mt. xxvii. 23</sub> cried out: "No, punish him in the Roman fashion! Stretch him on the cross!" Pilate heard them out, <sub>21</sub> and said to the chief priests: "Well, as you will! But you have a custom at the feast of the Passover to pardon one condemned malefactor. Well, I have lying in prison, Barabbas, a murderer and rioter. Which one of the two must be let free:

Jesus or Barabbas?"

Pilate thus wished to save Jesus; but the chief priests had so worked upon the people, that all cried out: "Barabbas, Barabbas!"

Mt. xxvii. 25   And Pilate said: "And what shall be done with Jesus?"

They again cried out: "Roman fashion,—to the cross, to the cross with him."

23   And Pilate tried to talk them over. He said: "Why do you press so hardly on him? He has done nothing that he should be punished with death, and he has done you no harm. I will set

Jn. xix. 4 him free, because I find no fault in him."

6   The chief priests and their servants cried out: "Crucify, crucify him!"

And Pilate said to them: "If so, then take him and crucify him yourselves. But I see no fault in him."

7   The chief priests answered: "We ask only that which our law demands. By our law, he must be executed for having made himself out to be Son of God."

8   When Pilate heard this word, he was troubled, because he did not know what this term

"Son of God" meant. And having returned into <sub></sub> Jn. xix. 9
the court, Pilate called up Jesus again, and asked
him: "Who are you, and whence are you?"

But Jesus did not answer.

Then Pilate said: "But why do you not     10
answer me? You surely see that you are in my
power, and that I can crucify you, or set you
free."

Jesus answered him: "You have no power.     11
There is power only from above."

Pilate, nevertheless, wished to set Jesus     12
free, and he said to them: "How is it you wish to     13
crucify your king?"

But the Jews said to him: "If you set Jesus     12
free, you will thereby show that you are a disloyal
servant to Caesar, because he who sets himself
up as king is an enemy to Caesar. Our king is     15
Caesar; but crucify this man."

And when Pilate heard these words, he     13
understood that he could now no longer refuse
to execute Jesus.

Then Pilate went out before the Jews, took     Mt. xxvii. 24
some water, washed his hands, and said: "I am
not guilty of the blood of this just man." And the

Mt. xxvii. 25   whole people cried out: "Let his blood be upon us and all our children."

Lk. xxiii. 23   So that the chief priests gained the upper

Jn. xix. 13   hand. And Pilate sat in his place of judgment,

Mt. xxvii. 26   and ordered Jesus to be first flogged.

28, 29   When they had flogged him, the soldiers, who had done this, put a crown upon his head and a rod in his hand, and threw a red cloak over his back, and fell to reviling him; in mockery, they bowed down to his feet, and said: "Hail, king of the Jews!" And others struck him on the cheeks, over the face, and spat in his face.

Jn. xix. 15   But the chief priests cried: "Crucify him! Our king is Caesar! Crucify him!"

16   And Pilate bade him be crucified.

Mt. xxvii. 31   Then they stripped Jesus of the red dress, put on him his own clothing, and bade him bear the cross to a place called Golgotha, there to be

Jn. xix. 18   crucified at once. And he carried his cross, and so came to Golgotha. And there they stretched Jesus on the cross, beside two other men. These two were at the sides, and Jesus was in the middle.

Lk. xxiii. 34   When they had crucified Jesus, he said:

"Father! forgive them; they do not know what they are doing."

And when Jesus was hung on the cross, Lk. xxiii. 35 the people thronged round him and railed at him. They came up, wagged their heads at him, Mk. xv. 29 and said: "So, you wish to destroy the temple of Jerusalem, and to build it up again in three days. Well now, save yourself, come down from the 30 cross!" And the chief priests and leaders stood 31 there also, and mocked at him, and said: "He thought to save others, but cannot save himself. Now show that you are Christ; come down from 32 the cross, and then we will believe you. He said that he was the Son of God, and that God would not forsake him. But how is it that God has now forsaken him?" And the people, and the chief priests, and the soldiers, railed at him, and even one of the robbers crucified with him, he too railed at him.

One of the robbers, reviling him, said: "If Lk. xxiii. 39 you are Christ, save yourself and us."

But the other robber heard this and said: 40 "Do you not fear God? You who are yourself on the cross, do you even rail at the innocent? You

Lk. xxiii. 41   and I are executed for our deserts, but this man has done no harm."

42   And, turning to Jesus, this robber said to him: "Lord, remember me in your kingdom."

43   And Jesus said to him: "Even now you are blessed with me!"

Mt. xxvii. 46   But at the ninth hour, Jesus, worn out, cried aloud: "Eloi, Eloi, lama sabachthani!" This means: "My God, my God! why hast Thou forsaken me?"

47   And when the people heard this, they began to say jeeringly: "He is calling the prophet Elias! Let us see whether Elias will come!"

Jn. xix. 28   Afterward, Jesus cried out: "Let me drink!"

And a man took a sponge, soaked it in vinegar, that stood by, and gave it to Jesus on a reed.

30   Jesus sucked the sponge, and cried out in a loud voice: "It is finished! Father, I give up my

Lk. xxiii. 46   spirit into your hands!" And, letting his head fall, he gave up the ghost.